Teacher's Guide for

HINENI EXPRESS

By Ellen J. Rank

BEHRMAN HOUSE

Behrman House, Inc.

www.behrmanhouse.com

Design: AURAS Design
Project Editor: Ann D. Koffsky

Springfield, NJ 07081
www.behrmanhouse.com
ISBN 978-0-87441-947-4

PRINTED IN THE UNITED STATES OF AMERICA

Visit www.behrmanhouse.com/hineni-express for more resources.

CONTENTS

INTENT AND PURPOSE OF HINENI EXPRESS

Hineni–the Hebrew word for "here I am"– is also used to express our readiness and willingness to perform a special task. In the Book of Exodus, when God calls to Moses from the burning bush, Moses responds, "*Hineni.*" So, too, your learners are ready to take on a new holy task, that of learning Hebrew prayer.

Hineni Express, a digest of all three volumes of the *Hineni: The New Hebrew Through Prayer* series, offers a new, streamlined vehicle for teaching Hebrew prayer. With a friendly "Let's get down to business" approach, *Hineni Express* takes learners on a quick and direct route to becoming knowledgeable and comfortable with Hebrew prayer.

The design and content of *Hineni Express* is targeted for 10-13 year-olds who, for a variety of reasons, are first introduced to reading Hebrew prayer in fifth grade or up. *Hineni Express* retains select key elements of the original series while incorporating new features to better meet the needs of these learners and to quickly give them the tools to confidently lead and participate in prayer services as they become *b'nei mitzvah*.

Hineni Express is ideal for classrooms, tutoring, and private learning. It is well suited to learners who have studied Modern Hebrew as well as those who began their Hebrew studies after fourth grade.

New in Hineni Express

New features in *Hineni Express* include:

- the full text for a number of prayers, such as מַעֲרִיב עֲרָבִים, that were abbreviated in the original series
- a chart listing the Shabbat morning prayers
- additional thought questions geared to bringing greater personal meaning and understanding to the prayer or blessing

Preserved in Hineni Express

As in *Hineni: The New Hebrew Through Prayer* series, the goal of *Hineni Express* is fluent siddur reading and an understanding of the key prayers in the Shabbat morning service, selections from the Friday evening service, and many blessings. Learners will understand the key words and roots and be able to discuss the concept of each prayer in English.

Hineni Express provides opportunities for learners to explore and reflect on Jewish values. It helps learners to understand the relevance and importance of the prayers in their lives, as well as the ethical values associated with each prayer.

Through *Hineni Express*, learners are prepared to be skilled, involved members of the Jewish community with a deep appreciation of Jewish values and a sense of belonging to a great people–*Am Yisrael*.

WHO SHOULD USE HINENI EXPRESS?

Middle Schoolers

Hineni Express is ideal for middle schoolers. While every learner is unique, those for whom *Hineni Express* is designed can be divided into three main groups:

- Learners who first begin their Hebrew education in fifth or sixth grade
- Students who are introduced to Hebrew through an active oral-aural approach
- Students with decoding difficulty who would benefit from starting over in prayer mastery

The streamlined format and content support quick learning, which is perfect for middle schoolers who will soon be preparing to become *b'nei mitzvah*. *Hineni Express* also is a great choice for learners studying privately or being tutored for extra individual support.

Children with Special Needs

Hineni Express is a great tool for teaching prayer to children with special needs. The focused streamlined content of *Hineni Express* allows learners to focus on essential elements and concepts. Techniques for using *Hineni Express* with learners who have learning challenges are found on page 17.

STRUCTURE OF THIS TEACHER'S GUIDE

The first part of this Teacher's Guide provides general background, techniques, and strategies for teaching *Hineni Express*.

The second part of this Teacher's Guide provides specific background and suggestions for each of the 15 lessons in *Hineni Express*. Each lesson overview includes:

- **About the Prayer**–a brief description of the prayers or blessings presented in the lesson, meaning and key concepts of the prayer, and its history or source.
- An **Essential Question(s)** related to the prayer that learners can go back to and reflect on as they learn more about the Shabbat prayers.
- **Learning Objectives** to help set learning goals for each lesson.
- **New Words and Phrases**–a comprehensive list of key prayer words and their relevant Word Cards. (Word Cards are from the original three-volume *Hineni* series.)
- **Introducing the Lesson**–an induction to the lesson's central ideas.
- **Roots**–identifies the root letters or key prayer words.
- **Bringing the Prayer/Blessing to Life**–choreography associated with the prayer.
- **Where We Are**–focuses on the placement of the prayer in the Shabbat service.

Keep in mind that many of the activities suggested for a specific prayer can be adapted to use with other prayers.

Answer sheets to the *Hineni Express* exercises can be found at www.behrmanhouse.com/hineni-express

TEACHING WITH HINENI EXPRESS

Lesson Contents

Each lesson typically includes:

- an introduction to one or more prayers or blessings and the main concept
- the Hebrew text of the prayers or blessings, including any **Prayer Variations**
- an English translation for the prayers or blessings
- a **Prayer Dictionary** with key words
- exercises to reinforce comprehension of the key words and the meaning of the prayers or blessings
- questions to bring personal connection and meaning to the prayers or blessings
- where the prayers or blessings fall in the service or home ritual (**Where We Are**)
- an associated short biblical or rabbinic text study (**From the Text**)
- choreography related to the prayers or blessings (**Prayer in Motion**)

Time Management

Your learners are poised to learn Hebrew prayer quickly. Motivated by their upcoming bar or bat mitzvah ceremony, many learners will recognize the importance of Hebrew reading and being able to fluently recite prayers and blessings. Given that your learners have limited time to master prayers and blessings prior to their bar or bat mitzvah, you will need to carefully plan—at the beginning of the year—goals for your learners to work toward this year.

There are a variety of factors you will need to consider as you map out your year:

- your learners' previous experience with Hebrew
- how many days a week your class meets
- how many hours each week can be devoted to Hebrew prayer

Most importantly, you will need to ascertain which prayers and blessings *b'nei mitzvah* are expected to lead. Generally, congregations will have a prioritized list of prayers and blessings for *b'nei mitzvah*. For example, a congregation may want all learners to be able to fluently recite *V'ahavta*. Only after they have mastered *V'ahavta*, will they learn *Yotzeir Or*. Ask your education director for a list of recommended prayers and blessings, and the order of priority.

As you plan the year, estimate about how long you think it will take learners to become comfortable with a prayer and to gain an understanding of the meaning of the prayer. Learners do not need to gain total fluency before you introduce a new prayer or blessing. They will have opportunities to become more fluent as they practice reading in class and at home as well as when they recite the prayer as part of class, school, or congregational services.

As you plan each lesson, decide which exercises are essential for your learners. Based on the goals and abilities of the learners, you may decide to omit or choose selections from certain exercises for your lesson. For example, if vocabulary acquisition is not central, you might omit or adapt activities based on prayer vocabulary.

Planning a Lesson

As you plan, remember that it is helpful to have some established routines and it is equally important to use different modalities for learning. While attention spans vary among learners, educators often estimate the average attention span being equal to the child's age plus or minus one minute. If you are teaching eleven- or twelve-year-olds, expect to change the mode of learning at least every ten minutes. This includes shifting between frontal, small group, and individual learning as well as between kinesthetic, aural, and visual learning.

Decide ahead of time which activities are most helpful and necessary for each learner. Identify what is essential for all learners as well as lesson components that can be reserved as enrichment for more advanced readers. Making this type of differentiated instruction regularized in your lessons will allow for quicker as well as deeper learning.

Setting the Stage

Create a space in your room to display a chart of the Shabbat morning prayers (see page 94 in the student text). You may wish to display a complete chart at the beginning of the year, or you may prefer to add each prayer to the chart as your class studies that prayer. It is also important to display an *alef-bet* chart and Hebrew vowel chart in your classroom for easy reference.

Before beginning *Hineni Express*, send an e-mail to parents describing what they and their child should expect. Mention, for example, how often learners will be using *Hineni Express* in class or if you will be asking learners to practice reading prayers and blessings at home. And, of course, let parents know the best way for them to contact you with any questions or concerns they might have.

Draw learners' attention to the title of the book, *Hineni Express*. Explain that *Hineni*, הִנֵּנִי, means, "Here I am." Ask learners when they might say, "Here I am." Tell learners about the first time the reply הִנֵּנִי is used in the Torah, how Abraham was the first person to answer הִנֵּנִי when God called upon him. His answer indicated his readiness to serve God (Genesis 22: 1-3). Generations later, God called to Moses from the burning bush. Again, the answer was הִנֵּנִי (Exodus 3: 1-4), and Moses served God by leading the children of Israel out of Egypt.

Invite learners to browse through the text. Ask: Based on what you see in *Hineni Express*, what are some things you are ready to do? (Answers may include: learn more prayers, become a better Hebrew reader, or learn when to bow during a prayer.)

Explain that "Express" reflects that they will be learning a lot of prayers in a short amount of time.

Introducing Prayer Concepts

Each lesson overview in this Teacher's Guide opens with **About the Prayer**. This element includes key concepts for each of the prayers and blessings. As you plan your lessons for each lesson, decide which of these concepts you will present to your learners and identify ways for them to delve into these concepts. Many of the key concepts are introduced through the activities and exercises in *Hineni Express*.

Essential Questions for the prayers and blessings are included in the overview for each lesson. Consider printing the lesson's question(s) on an 8½" × 11" page and displaying it in your room as you introduce your learners to a new lesson. You might leave each question on display throughout the year. This can serve as a visual reminder to learners and encourage them to think deeper about the questions and revisit them as they continue to recite the prayers they have learned and study new prayers.

STUDENT TEXT ELEMENTS THAT BUILD UNDERSTANDING OF THE PRAYER CONCEPTS

Introduction: Each lesson opens with an introduction that presents one or more key concepts of the prayer or blessing. Invite your learners to read the introduction and encourage them to ask any questions they might have about the reading. Most of the introductions to the prayers close with an open-ended question designed to give learners an opportunity to reflect on the prayer's key concepts.

Prayer Variations: Several prayers have variations that reflect the beliefs of a particular movement: Reform, Reconstructionist, or Conservative. As these variations are presented in the lessons, questions are often posed to give learners the opportunity to think deeper about a key concept in the prayer. For example, in the lesson on אָבוֹת וְאִמָּהוֹת, in "**Prayer Variations**" it is explained that "some congregations pray for God to bring a redeemer (גּוֹאֵל)–the Messiah–who will bring peace to the world, while other congregations pray for redemption (גְּאֻלָּה)–a state of peace and perfection in the world."

What's in a Name? Learners discuss how key concepts of certain prayers and blessings, such as גְּבוּרוֹת, relate to the name of the prayer or blessing.

Prayer in Motion: Discussion of choreography gives learners another gateway into understanding a key concept. When learners reflect on how many people cover their eyes when saying the שְׁמַע, learners are asked: How do you get yourself to focus and concentrate on something that is important in your life?

Where We Are: This section guides learners to recognize where a prayer is set in the service. This activity, too, provides an opportunity to reflect on a prayer's key concept. Recognizing, for example, that the בָּרְכוּ comes at the beginning of the service, can help learners to remember that the בָּרְכוּ is a call to prayer.

Prayer Dictionary: Key words often present clues to key concepts. For example, in שְׁמַע you might direct learners to look at the words יְיָ and אֶחָד in the **Prayer Dictionary** and ask them how these two key words support the Jewish belief in one God.

Prayer Building Blocks: Many of these exercises include thought questions designed to deepen the learners' understanding and appreciation of the prayer.

Open-ended Questions: Many lessons include open-ended questions that provide opportunities for discussing key concepts. For example, when studying the Mourners' Kaddish, learners are asked: Why do you think that a prayer praising God is recited in memory of a loved one?

INTRODUCING PRAYER VOCABULARY

A **Prayer Dictionary** of key prayer vocabulary words is presented for each prayer or set of blessings. Techniques for introducing and reinforcing the key vocabulary include:

- Direct learners to a key word in the **Prayer Dictionary.** Ask them to highlight the word in the dictionary. Call on a volunteer to say its meaning. Direct learners to find and highlight the word in the text of the prayer or blessing.
- Read a prayer aloud. Pause before a key word. Invite the class to read that word aloud chorally. Call on a volunteer to say its English meaning.
- Challenge learners to find, for example, a key word that has the letter *samech*. Call on a volunteer to read the word, or say where it is located in the prayer. Have the class chorally read the word and say its English meaning.
- Use a SMARTboard, chalkboard or Word Cards to display the key vocabulary words. Invite learners to identify various key words, such as words with the root letters קדשׁ.

Building Your Vocabulary: This section provides an opportunity for learners to gain fluency in reading key vocabulary words and to build their knowledge of key Hebrew prayer vocabulary. Learners are asked, for example, to identify the correct English meaning of a key word. See suggestions in Collaborative Learning for ways to present this activity.

Prayer Building Blocks: This section presents exercises that focus on the meaning of key words, root letters, prefixes, and suffixes. To support the learning of roots, prefixes, and suffixes, create a display in your classroom as described in the following paragraphs.

INTRODUCING WORD ROOTS

Roots: This provides opportunities for learners to learn the basic meaning of a variety of roots and to identify root letters of some key prayer words. *Hineni Express* introduces learners to several roots, including: ברכ, קדשׁ, זכר, מלכ, אהב, חיה, and עשׂה.

Create and display word trees to serve as visual reminders of key roots, words built on those roots, and the meaning of the roots. For each root, create a tree from poster board with three roots. On each of the three roots write one root letter (e.g., ב ר כ). Then write the meaning of the root ("bless," "praise") on the trunk of the tree. If possible, laminate the tree. As learners meet new words with this root (בָּרוּךְ, בָּרְכוּ), add these words onto the leafy part of the tree.

INTRODUCING PREFIXES AND SUFFIXES

Hineni Express introduces learners to a number of prefixes and suffixes. Activities to build learners knowledge of these prefixes and suffixes are found in **Prayer Building Blocks.** Consider creating a prefix chart and a suffix chart. When a new prefix or suffix is presented in the text, add the prefix or suffix to the chart, along with its English translation.

Building Prayer Fluency

ALEF-BET REVIEW

Begin the year with a thorough review of the letters and vowels in the Hebrew alphabet. Use an *alef-bet* poster, *alef-bet* flashcards, or Word Cards from the previous year. You can also use a transitional reading text such as the *Back-to-School Hebrew Reading Refresher* to review and drill Hebrew decoding before learners begin *Hineni Express.*

BUILDING WHOLE WORD RECOGNITION SKILLS

Decide ahead of time which words learners will practice reading as whole words. As each of these words appears in *Hineni Express*, devote time to having the learners read the whole word. Once a whole word can be easily identified, the learner should be able to fluently read the word without having to sound out each consonant and vowel.

Being able to identify and read a word provides a hook for learners to remember the sounds of individual letters and vowels. For example, many learners find it difficult to distinguish between צ and ע. In this case, you can choose a familiar word such as הָעוֹלָם, you show the class the whole word, focus on the second letter, and reinforce that ע is silent. You might have learners practice writing and saying הָעוֹלָם as they write each letter.

Reading in general becomes more fluent with greater whole word recognition. Think about how you read English. If you had to phonetically sound out each word, reading would be very tedious. And so it is for the Hebrew reader.

Techniques for building whole word recognition include quick activities using Word Cards or key words that are displayed. For example, display seven or eight key words. Ask learners to close their eyes as you remove one of the words. Call on a volunteer to name the word that was removed. For an extra challenge, ask the volunteer to say the English meaning.

To encourage whole word recognition, engage learners in a game in which they gain points for reading a word correctly *and* earn an extra point if they can recognize the word and read it without decoding.

Writing out a word can help learners to become more familiar with the letters and vowels of a particular word. This familiarity can boost the learner's skill in reading the word. Consider having a set of mini-whiteboards available to your learners. These can be used in a variety of ways. For example, learners can practice writing and reading key words individually or with a partner. You could say the English meaning of a key word and ask learners, using the **Prayer Dictionary** for reference, to write and then read the key word. Note that these mini-whiteboards provide great opportunities for formative assessment (see page 15).

BUILDING DECODING SKILLS

It is important for new readers to hear the correct pronunciation of words before they try to sound them out by themselves. Read the words of a prayer or blessing to your learners, having learners follow along in the textbook and echo what you have read. Vary the way you read the words so that learners are looking at the reading. Suggestions include:

- Read one to three words at a time, varying the number as you go along. Learners should echo those one to three words.
- After learners have echoed the words, chant the words, then have learners chant them with you.

After learners have heard and practiced a line or two of the prayer or blessing, direct learners to take turns reading with a partner.

Additional suggestions for reading practice to build prayer fluency include:

- Have learners work in small groups practicing one line at a time. Groups move on to practice the new line once everyone in the group can read the first line.
- Call on various groups, such as learners wearing green or those born in the summer, to read a particular line.
- Go around the room, having learners, or a pair of learners, each read one or two words.
- Direct the entire class to read a word after you say where they will find it. For example, ask them to read the third word on line four or the word in line three that begins with ל.

To keep learners engaged, remember to vary the activity at least every ten minutes.

REINFORCING PRAYER AWARENESS

Begin each class with a short (two- to five-minute) class service, a recap of the prayers and blessings learned to date. Ask individual learners to take turns as leaders. Consider using your congregation's siddur. This will help learners become familiar and comfortable with the siddur that they will be using at congregational services.

As your learners master more of the prayers, you may choose to alternate which prayers you include in your class service. This will allow learners to review and practice different prayers in only a few minutes of each class session. You may choose to end the service by having the class recite the blessing for engaging in study:

בָּרוּךְ אַתָּה, יְיָ אֱלֹהֵינוּ, מֶלֶךְ הָעוֹלָם, אֲשֶׁר קִדְּשָׁנוּ בְּמִצְוֹתָיו, וְצִוָּנוּ לַעֲסוֹק בְּדִבְרֵי תוֹרָה.

Praised are You, Adonai our God, Ruler of the world, who makes us holy with commandments, and commands us to engage in the study of Torah.

Baruch Atah, Adonai Eloheinu, Melech ha'olam, asher kideshanu b'mitzvotav v'tzivanu la'asokb'divrei Torah.

HOMEWORK

Review and practice at home will help learners hone the Hebrew decoding skills and vocabulary they acquire in school. However, whether or not to assign homework is a decision best made by your school administration. For more on ways to extend the learning into the home, see page 15.

Collaborative Learning

Collaborative learning is a method of teaching in which learners work together so that everyone, not just themselves, achieves a certain goal. Learning is collaborative rather than competitive. Examples include learners helping one another to complete an exercise in the text or coaching one another on reading new words.

In an environment that supports collaborative learning:

- Learners must feel safe in your classroom. They need to know that their classmates will treat them with respect and that it is okay to say that they don't know something or that they need help.
- Collaborative learning works best when the teacher decides the members of each group. Balance the group, considering academic as well as social-emotional factors.
- Groups are small enough to allow for everyone to participate actively.
- Tasks are clearly defined for learners.
- Each learner knows what to do. Consider assigning "jobs" to different group members. For example, one group member can be assigned the job of reporting the group's answers to the class.

Collaborative learning promotes a more relaxed atmosphere in the class and can make learning much more engaging and fun. Another important aspect of collaborative Learning is that it helps learners to develop their interpersonal skills and to build relationships with classmates. As we become more and more aware of the importance of creating and building relationships within our community, we can better understand the role and impact of employing Collaborative Learning in the classroom.

It is helpful to think of collaborative learning as a three-step process:

1. Present the task to the learners.
2. Learners work collaboratively on the task. Be sure to provide sufficient time for learners to successfully complete the task. Walk around, checking in on groups, as they are working.
3. Debrief. Ask for a few volunteers to share the results of their learning

USING COLLABORATIVE LEARNING TO BUILD HEBREW PRAYER SKILLS

Think-Pair-Share: This method allows for independent thinking, short review with a partner, and then checking for accuracy with the full class. To use Think-Pair-Share with *Hineni Express:*

- Direct learners to independently complete a short exercise in *Hineni Express.*
- After a few minutes, have learners turn to a partner and compare their work and agree on a shared answer.
- Lastly, invite volunteers to share their answers with the whole class.

You might, for example, use Think-Pair-Share in a **Building Your Vocabulary** exercise when learners are asked to identify the English meaning of a key Hebrew prayer word.

Jigsaw: Jigsaw allows learners to master a select amount of information and to then share their expertise with others. The following collaborative learning is a variation on the established Jigsaw method.

- Divide class into small teams.
- Assign each team a specific task, such as reading a specific line of a prayer. Allow the team time for all learners to master the reading. Team members work together coaching one another with the reading.
- Direct learners to move from their expert team to their mixed team. Each person in the new mixed team will be an expert on a specific line from the prayer. Teams then practice reading the lines with the experts who help one another master the reading.

Here is an example of expert and mixed teams.

Expert Team 1		Expert Team 2		Expert Team 3		Expert Team 4	
1 Sarah	1 Ariana	2 David	2 Jacob	3 Rachel	3 Emma	4 Michael	4 Daniel
1 Aiden	1 Max	2 Sophie	2 Sydney	3 Jonah	3 Nathan	4 Paula	4 Lara

Mixed Team A		Mixed Team B		Mixed Team C		Mixed Team D	
1 Sarah	2 David	1 Ariana	2 Jacob	1 Aiden	2 Sophie	1 Max	2 Sydney
3 Rachel	4 Michael	3 Emma	4 Daniel	3 Jonah	4 Paula	3 Nathan	4 Lara

HEVRUTA READING

Create a personalized prayer reading chart for each learner. Hevruta (partners) work to help one another gain fluency and accuracy in their mastery of reading words and lines from prayers. Here is an example of a page to give a learner:

Dear Hannah,
Here is your very own Hebrew reading plan. Below is a list of:

- prayers and blessings you will be studying
- the page and lines in Hineni Express to practice reading

Take turns with your hevruta, helping one another learn to read these lines from prayers. Once you feel confident reading the line, ask your hevruta to sign that you can accurately read the line. If your hevruta isn't sure of how to read the line, you may ask me or another classmate to check your reading and to write the date you have mastered the reading.

Name of prayer or blessing	Page in *Hineni Express*	Line(s)	Checked by	Date
קִדּוּשׁ	12	1-2		
	12	3-5		
	12	6-8		

Classroom Games

Games can add variety and energy to your classroom. They reinforce learning and capture learners' attention through a fun, lively medium. As you plan to use the games below, or others you may develop or choose to use, keep the following considerations in mind:

- Choose games that contribute to improving specific skills and reading fluency–games that have pedagogic value.
- Use games that move quickly. Don't spend more time on a game than it deserves.
- Stop when learners' interest begins to wane.
- Choose games appropriate to the age group.
- Use games that are easy to follow and organize. Explain rules clearly. Avoid complicated directions. You want learners' attention focused on the skills being reinforced, not on rules.
- Maintain control of the class.
- When playing a game with the entire class, make sure that all learners are actively involved and can experience success.

CONCENTRATION

Create two sets of cards: one with Hebrew words and one with the English translation. Place all cards, word-side up, on the floor or a large table. Then turn the cards over so that the blank sides face up. Ask learners individually (or in teams) to try to match the pairs by turning any two cards over. If they match, award the player (or team) the matched pair of cards. If they do not match, place the cards back in their original position, word side down, and ask another learner (or the other team) to go. Continue the game until all cards have been removed. The player or team with the most matches wins.

TIC-TAC-TOE

Draw a Tic-Tac-Toe diagram on the board. Divide learners into two teams, X and O. Show a Word Card, then call on a learner from Team X to read the Hebrew word. If the learner reads the word correctly, ask him or her to place an X in one of the squares. Then it is Team O's turn; show another Word Card, and call on a learner from Team O to read it. If the learner reads the word correctly, ask him or her to place an O in one of the squares. The team that marks three in a row across, down, or diagonally is the winning team. *Variations include:* Learners read the word on the Word Card and the sentence (or line) in the prayer passage that contains the word before placing a mark in a square; Learners read the Hebrew and give the English meaning before placing a mark in a square; Learners answer questions about the prayer passage(s) in order to place a mark in a square.

PASS THE BALL

Ask the class to stand in a circle. Toss the ball to a learner and show them a key word. The learner-catcher reads the word and/or says its English meaning, and tosses the ball to another learner. Teacher shows key word to next learner-catcher.

USING THE DIGITAL COMPANION

Hineni Express is available with a digital companion in the Online Learning Center. Your education director will set up the digital space for your class, and your students can begin using *Hineni Express OLC Edition* for at-home prayer practice right away. The digital companion has been designed to reinforce reading fluency and vocabulary use introduced in the book and in class. The online practice material extends the amount of Hebrew learning time into the home. Parents do not need to read Hebrew themselves for their children to use the digital companion!

The digital companion gives students a clear, fun way to practice regularly at home content they started to explore in school. Hebrew reading is a skill, and brain-based research shows that even five minutes a day of practice will lead to increased confidence and stronger skills compared to not practicing or even to practicing during a single but much longer session.

Online Review Activities

The *Hineni Express OLC Edition* groups the prayers and blessings into six categories–Home Observance, Opening Prayers, Amidah, Prayers for Peace, Torah Service, and Concluding Prayers. Students can listen to the Hebrew text of each prayer one word or one line at a time, or in its entirety. They can also record themselves reading the prayers, either one word or phrase at a time, or in its entirety. At the end of each group of prayers, students can play online games that use the Hebrew words of the prayer.

Creating an Environment for Success

To help students get the most out of the resources of the digital companion, teachers need to reinforce its use. The following strategies can help you use the *Hineni Express OLC Edition* effectively with your students:

- **Set expectations.** Expect students to do their practice work at home, and reinforce that it's not optional. Make this clear to families at the start of the school year and keep parents in the loop about how often their children are practicing, and the results they achieve when they do.
- **Build comfort level for all users.** Demonstrate for students how to sign into the OLC and have all students log in during class to ensure everyone knows how to access the class page. Hold an open house to familiarize parents with the OLC and share how they can encourage their children at home. As a teacher, do the lessons yourself so you are very familiar with the content you're assigning.
- **Encourage home use.** Use the tools in the OLC to create fun posts and short contests, provide videos from YouTube, and provide other enticements to encourage students to log in. Once they are in they are more likely to practice.
- **Reward use.** Kids like to be acknowledged. Recognize students' at-home use and show them you're paying attention. Give stickers or prizes for high usage, highlight class participation on a poster on the door, or consider friendly competitions between classes or among students. Show evidence of success to keep the energy going!
- **Track progress.** What gets measured, gets done! It's easy to track student progress in the OLC using the Assessment button right on your class page. Report back to class on how they're doing.

Visit the OLC section of the Behrman House website for instructions on how to set up the Online Learning Center and monitor student progress.

ASSESSMENT

Assessment enables both you and your learners to gain a clear understanding of where each learner is in the learning process and what the next steps should be. Assessment is primarily a process for helping learners grow and learn. It can also help you to plan future lessons; to check how well you are helping learners build their skills, understanding, and appreciation of prayer; and to consider the most effective activities and discussions for your group of learners.

The Partnership of Learning Objectives, Lesson Planning, and Assessment

STEP 1: IDENTIFY LEARNING OBJECTIVES

Each lesson overview includes a listing of learning objectives. Before you design your lesson plans, you will need to decide which learning objectives are essential for your learners. Feel free to adapt the learning objectives to better meet the needs of your own class.

STEP 2: LESSON PLANNING

Review the lesson overview in this Teacher's Guide and the full lesson in *Hineni Express*. Your lesson plans should align with the learning objectives. Decide which parts of the text will be presented to your learners. Estimate how much time they will need to learn about the new prayer and gain fluency in reading the prayer.

STEP 3: ASSESSMENT

As you plan your lesson, be sure to include assessment. Look back at each of the learning objectives and plan how you can assess how well learners are reaching that objective. Assessment can be:

- **Formative** – a process that enables both the teacher and learner to recognize what the learner has achieved and to use that information to plan and modify the current lesson to best meet the learner's needs. Formative assessment can be formal, such as when you listen to a learner to judge reading fluency of a particular line in a prayer. It can also be informal. You might, for example, observe learners as they play concentration with a partner and assess learners' ability to read the Hebrew and identify the English translation.
- **Summative** – takes place at the end of a unit to assess and summarize what the learner has achieved. This assessment could be, for example, a written quiz about key words and concepts, or performance based – observing a learner lead the class in reciting a particular prayer.

The following is an example of the partnership of learning objective, lesson planning and assessment: A lesson objective in Lesson 6 is for learners to categorize the מִי כָמֹכָה as a prayer of praise, request, or thanks. A learner's ability to identify a prayer as one of praise, request, or thanks can be assessed when learners complete the exercise on page 34 of the student book. This exercise asks learners to respond to the following: Do you think the מִי כָמֹכָה is a prayer of praise, a prayer of asking for something, or a prayer of thanks? As you plan your lesson, decide how and when you will present this exercise to your learners.

Prayer Mastery Assessment Chart

Consider creating a chart to assess each learner's reading fluency and comprehension of the prayer, key words, and phrases. Keep a record of the learner's progress by writing a comment and dating the chart after each assessment is complete. Keep the charts in a dedicated folder or binder.

As learners are working on class activities independently, with partners, or in small groups, meet individually with learners to assess their reading fluency and knowledge of prayer content.

Here is an example of a prayer mastery assessment chart. (*A customizable version of this chart can be found at: www.behrmanhouse.com/hineni-express*)

Reads prayer fluently	Explains meaning of prayer	Understands key words and phrases		
			בְּרָכוֹת	1
			בְּרָכוֹת שֶׁל שַׁבָּת	2
			בְּרָכוֹת שֶׁל יוֹם טוֹב	3
			קִדּוּשׁ	4
			בָּרְכוּ	5

Ongoing assessment will help you track whether learners are mastering the material and allow you to plan remediation accordingly. If you hear that a learner has difficulty with three consecutive words or five words in a line, stop the assessment and remediate. For example, allow the learner to practice this item with a classroom aide or the resource room tutor. If the learner demonstrates reading fluency, have the learner continue reading each set of words for the lessons the class has studied.

Assessments can reveal areas that warrant additional practice. If you see that several learners are having difficulty with the same item, a classroom or small group review may be beneficial.

WORKING EFFECTIVELY WITH LEARNERS WITH LEARNING CHALLENGES

All children learn and develop differently. Teachers can serve their learners best by recognizing each child's individual strengths and specific learning challenges. Consult with your school's director to learn about each learner's specific learning needs.

Remember, learners may fall into more than one category and will benefit from a combination of strategies. Above all, embrace your learners, knowing that each is created *b'tzelem Elohim* (in God's image). While these strategies are geared toward learners with learning challenges, all learners can benefit from the techniques and modifications listed below:

Build Relationships with and among Your Learners

- Reach out before school starts by sending home a letter or e-mail, or by calling to introduce yourself to your learners.
- Begin the year with a "get-to-know-you" game and by having learners individually complete an "All about Me" page.
- Establish that fair doesn't necessarily mean equal; fair means that every learner gets what he or she needs to be successful.
- Incorporate trust-building activities into your class's everyday lessons and routines. Cooperative learning and classroom discussion can provide opportunities for learners to build relationships and trust.

Techniques for Learners with Specific Learning Challenges

- **For Learners with Attention Issues:** Seat the learner close to you and minimize distractions. Repeat directions. Privately establish a refocusing system with the learner, such as a gentle tap on the shoulder or approaching his or her desk. Help learners organize their papers and supplies. Provide an extra copy of *Hineni Express* for use at home. Ensure homework assignments are written down.
- **For Learners with Auditory Processing Issues:** Minimize noise and distractions. Have the learner repeat directions back to you to ensure understanding. Provide learners with a written copy of verbal instructions.
- **For Learners with Visual Processing Difficulty**: Read written directions aloud. For individual seatwork, allow the learner to work with a *madrich(ah)* or classmate to read the information aloud. Have the learner use an index card to track the line being read or cover the portion of the page not being worked on. Be willing to provide an alternative activity such as highlighting instead of circling key vocabulary.
- **For Learners with Emotional Concerns:** Establish your classroom as a safe space for learning and building relationships by letting learners know that they are each valued and that everyone will be treated with kindness and respect. Allow learners to participate in choral reading, rather than reading aloud individually. Assess learners individually until they feel more confident. Provide positive reinforcement regularly to boost self-esteem.
- **For Learners Who Have Behavioral Challenges:** Set firm but reasonable expectations. Minimize transitions such as changing activities abruptly, and inform learners of schedule changes. Maintain a positive relationship with parents, for example, by returning messages promptly. Find out what works for the learner at home and in secular school to mirror in your own classroom where possible.

LESSON SUMMARIES

LESSON 1 • בְּרָכוֹת

TEXT PAGES 4-11

About the Prayer

A בְּרָכָה is a blessing that praises and thanks God for specific spiritual and material gifts. Reciting a בְּרָכָה shows our appreciation for the world around us. The בְּרָכוֹת–"blessings"–express a direct relationship between the worshiper and God. Tradition teaches that God is both our partner and our Ruler.

Blessings of mitzvah–בְּרָכוֹת שֶׁל מִצְוָה–remind us that we are fulfilling מִצְוֹת, commandments in the Torah. These commandments lead us to actions that help us fulfill the greater commandment to be a holy people.

Some blessings are recited any day of the week. Others are specific to Shabbat or other holidays. Every Friday night we sanctify Shabbat with a special ceremony: we recite blessings over candles, wine, and bread. Shabbat is a day set aside for rest from our weekday activities–it is the sanctification of time.

Each יוֹם טוֹב–Jewish holiday–has its own traditions and blessings. The blessings we recite are an expression of our appreciation for the good in our lives. We recite blessings for specific holiday *mitzvot*, such as hearing the shofar, lighting a Hanukkah Menorah, and eating matzah on Pesach.

Traditionally we recite a blessing before engaging in the related act. For example, we say the blessing over fruit before eating a fruit and the blessing for sitting in the sukkah before we sit.

Essential Question

How can reciting blessings strengthen our connection to the Jewish people, and help us appreciate the world around us?

Learning Objectives

Learners will be able to:

- Identify the six words that always appear at the beginning of a blessing and the ten words that always appear at the beginning of a blessing for a mitzvah.
- Recite blessings said over different foods, before various *mitzvot*, and on Shabbat and holidays.
- Define key words found in and related to blessings.
- Identify and say the meaning of the root letters קדשׁ and ברכ.
- Recognize that words with the root קדשׁ have "holy" or "set apart" as part of their meaning, and that words with the root ברכ have "blessed" or "praised" as part of their meaning.

New Words and Phrases

(Note: Related Word Cards from the 3-volume *Hineni* series are indicated in parentheses. H=*Hineni*; 1, 2, and 3=Volume, #=Word Card #. Example: H1#7= *Hineni*, Volume 1, Word Card #7)

חֲנֻכָּה (H1#57)	הַגָּפֶן (H1#48)	שֶׁהֶחֱיָנוּ (H1#60)	בָּרוּךְ (H1#4)
נִסִּים (H1#58)	הַמּוֹצִיא (H1#49)	אֲשֶׁר (H1#38)	אַתָּה (H1#35)
בַּזְּמַן הַזֶּה (H1#59)	לֶחֶם (H1#50)	קִדְּשָׁנוּ (H1#39)	יְיָ (H1#2)
אֲכִילַת (H1#62)	מִן (H1#51)	בְּמִצְוֹתָיו (H1#40)	אֱלֹהֵינוּ (H1#19)
מַצָּה (H1#63)	הָאָרֶץ (H1#52)	וְצִוָּנוּ (H1#41)	מֶלֶךְ (H1#36)
מָרוֹר (H1#64)	עֵץ (H1#53)	לְהַדְלִיק (H1#42)	הָעוֹלָם (H1#37)
	שׁוֹפָר (H1#54)	נֵר (H1#43)	בּוֹרֵא (H1# 46)
	בַּסֻּכָּה (H1#55)	שֶׁל (H1#44)	פְּרִי (H1#47)
	לוּלָב (H1#56)	שַׁבָּת (H1#45)	הָאֲדָמָה (H1#61)

Introducing the Lesson

Ask: What are some things you do when you receive a gift? (*Answers may include: say thank you, write a thank you note, show the gift to others*)
Why do you do or say these things? (*Answers may include: to show appreciation, it's polite, so the person who gave the gift knows I like it*)

According to our tradition, we also receive gifts from God, such as the food we eat. There are special blessings, בְּרָכוֹת, that are recited when we are about to use one of these gifts. That is our way of saying thank you for this gift.

Invite learners to name blessings that might be said on Shabbat and holidays. List suggestions on the board. Explain that some of these blessings are recited over specific מִצְוֹת, actions that, according to our tradition, God has commanded us to perform. Tell learners that in this lesson they will learn to recite blessings said on many different occasions.

Bringing the Prayer to Life

Incorporate the blessings into your classroom routine whenever possible. For example, have volunteers take turns leading the class in the blessing over baked goods if you are having a class snack. Consider celebrating *havdalah* as part of your weekly routine. According to tradition, *havdalah* can be recited anytime from Saturday night until sunset on Tuesday. You might have each learner make their own spice bag to use during *havdalah*. You'll also need a *havdalah* candle and grape juice. *Havdalah* is a great sensory experience that your learners will remember.

LESSON 2 • קִדּוּשׁ

TEXT PAGES 12-16

About the Prayer

The Hebrew word קִדּוּשׁ means "sanctification," "making holy," or "setting apart." A commandment in the Torah tells us to "remember the Sabbath day and keep it holy." (Exodus 20: 8) One of the ways we perform this commandment is by reciting the קִדּוּשׁ.

Shabbat is considered a time of joy ("If you call the Sabbath a joy, God's holy day is honored" [Isaiah 58: 13]), and wine is a symbol of joy ("Wine makes glad the human heart," [Psalms 104: 15]) and so we recite the קִדּוּשׁ with wine on Shabbat.

The קִדּוּשׁ is recited both in synagogue and in the home. One explanation for this custom of reciting it in synagogue is that long ago synagogues also served as Jewish hostels. Travelers and visitors would spend the night in a side room, eating their meals as well as sleeping there. To be certain that they fulfilled the mitzvah of hearing קִדּוּשׁ, the congregation recited the prayer in the synagogue. Another possible explanation is that קִדּוּשׁ was recited in the synagogue so that poor people who could not afford wine at home would be able to fulfill this mitzvah at the synagogue.

Essential Question

What makes something holy?

Learning Objectives

Learners will be able to:

- Describe the two moments to remember–Creation and the Exodus (from Egypt)–mentioned in the קִדּוּשׁ for Shabbat and suggest why it is important for us to remember these events.
- Recite the קִדּוּשׁ.
- Define key words found in the קִדּוּשׁ.
- Identify and say the meaning of the root letters קדשׁ and זכר.
- Recognize that words with the root קדשׁ have "holy" or "set apart" as part of their meaning, and that words built on the root זכר have "remember" as part of their meaning.
- Identify the mitzvah of remembering Shabbat as one of the Ten Commandments.
- Reflect on what it means to be, or to make something, holy.
- Describe different traditions for reciting the Kiddush.

New Words and Phrases

קִדּוּשׁ (H1#65)
זִכָּרוֹן (H1#66)
(לְ)מַעֲשֵׂה בְרֵאשִׁית (H1#67)
זֵכֶר (H1#68)
(לִ)יצִיאַת מִצְרָיִם (H1#69)
בְּאַהֲבָה (H1#70)
וּבְרָצוֹן (H1#71)

Introducing the Lesson

As a class, brainstorm what learners know about the creation story told in Genesis. Write learners' suggestions on the board. Next, as a class create a list describing what learners know about the Israelites' exodus from Egypt. Encourage learners to tell or act out their favorite parts of these accounts. Feel free to add details to help learners recall these stories.

Explain to learners that they are about to learn the second blessing of the Shabbat Kiddush. This blessing tells how Shabbat is a memory of both the creation of the world and the Israelites' exodus from Egypt.

Remind learners that they have already learned the first blessing in the Shabbat Kiddush. Invite learners to recite the blessing over wine or grape juice.

Roots

To reinforce the concept of Hebrew roots:

- Create a root tree as follows: Cut a sheet of brown construction paper the shape of a tree trunk with three large roots. Cut a sheet of green construction paper the shape of a leafy tree top. Affix the trunk and the leafy top onto a bulletin board.
- Write ק ד שׁ on the roots – one letter on each root.
- Write the English meaning – holy – on the trunk.
- Write or affix the word קִדּוּשׁ on the green leafy top. Add, or invite learners to add, other the words from the קִדּוּשׁ with this same root: קִדְּשָׁנוּ-קָדְשׁוֹ-קֹדֶשׁ-קִדַּשְׁתָּ-קָדְשְׁךָ-מְקַדֵּשׁ.

Bringing the Blessing to Life

As your learners gain fluency in reciting the Kiddush, have them practice according to the traditions of your congregation. Model how the leader holds the filled Kiddush cup high as he or she chants the Kiddush. Invite your class to join in singing with you at the point your congregation traditionally joins in with the person leading the Kiddush. Learners should be standing or sitting – depending on your congregation's tradition.

Consider making Kiddush a part of your daily or weekly classroom service. Once learners become more fluent in reciting the Kiddush, have volunteers take turns leading the Kiddush. Most kids love to be the one who gets to drink the grape juice!

LESSON 3 • בָּרְכוּ
TEXT PAGES 17–20

About the Prayer

The בָּרְכוּ is a call to prayer, announcing that the prayer service is beginning. It is the official call to prayer in the morning and evening services. It summons the community–the congregation–to join together in prayer. Since the minyan, a group of ten or more Jews who are at least of bar or bat mitzvah age, represents the community as a whole, this ancient prayer is traditionally recited only when a minyan is present.

We trace this custom of calling the congregation together to worship back to the days of the Temple. (Nehemiah 9: 5) The בָּרְכוּ is also the beginning of the first blessing we recite when called to the Torah for an *aliyah*.

Essential Question

Why pray with a minyan?

Learning Objectives

Learners will be able to:

- Identify the בָּרְכוּ as the call to gather a community to prayer.
- Recite the בָּרְכוּ fluently.
- Define key words and the key root (ברכ) found in the בָּרְכוּ.
- Recognize various spellings for God's name.
- Explain that traditionally the בָּרְכוּ is only recited when a *minyan* is present.
- Discuss the tradition of praying with a *minyan*.
- Explain why the prayer is named בָּרְכוּ.
- Identify that the בָּרְכוּ is based on words from the Bible.
- Demonstrate the traditional choreography for the בָּרְכוּ.
- Locate the בָּרְכוּ in the Shabbat morning service.

New Words and Phrases

בָּרְכוּ (H1#1)
יְיָ (H1#2)
הַמְבֹרָךְ (H1#3)
בָּרוּךְ (H1#4)
לְעוֹלָם וָעֶד (H1#5)

Introducing the Lesson

Make a sound, for example by ringing a bell, to get your learners' attention. Ask: What are some ways that teachers, coaches, or friends let you and others know that a group activity is about to begin? (*turn lights on and off; clap hands; start a cheer*) Explain that a special prayer in our service, the בָּרְכוּ, signals to the congregation that the main part of the service is about to begin.

Roots

To reinforce the concept of Hebrew roots:

- Prepare a tree with roots as described on page 21.
- Write כ ר ב on the roots – one letter on each root.
- Write the English meaning – bless, praise – on the trunk.
- Write or affix the word בָּרְכוּ on the green leafy top. Add, or invite learners to add, other words with this same root: בָּרוּךְ - הַמְבֹרָךְ - בְּרָכוֹת-בְּרָכָה

You may wish to review that כּכך and בּב are family letters. Invite volunteers to point out words that have ךְ ,כּ ,כ and בּ ,ב as part of the word.

Bringing the Prayer to Life

As your learners gain fluency in reciting the בָּרְכוּ, integrate the בָּרְכוּ into your daily, or weekly, classroom service. Model how the leader bows on the word בָּרְכוּ. Remind learners that they in turn bow as they say the response. Model bowing as you repeat the response.

Once learners become more fluent in reciting the בָּרְכוּ, have volunteers take turns leading this call to prayer.

For Discussion: A Conversation about Why Pray with a Minyan

Explain that, while most prayers are intended to be recited privately or with a congregation, traditionally the בָּרְכוּ is only included in a prayer service in which a minyan is present. Ask learners to think about the meaning of the בָּרְכוּ and to explain why the בָּרְכוּ is not a private prayer. (*It is a dialogue between a leader and a group of people.*)

Divide the class into groups of 3–5 learners. Have each group list ways in which having prayers that require a minyan may help to build and support our Jewish community. (*People come together so others can say prayers; we meet others in our community when we come to synagogue; we help each other by attending a service so that there can be ten adults.*) Call on a representative from each group to read its list.

Ask: On what occasions might members of the Jewish community come together so *others* can say prayers? (*Times of sorrow such as a funeral so mourners can say Kaddish; times of joy or celebration such as a wedding*)

Where We Are

If you have a list displayed of the Shabbat blessings (see page 7, Setting the Stage), place a marker next to the בָּרְכוּ. If you will be adding the names of the prayers and blessings as they are studied, begin the list by writing or affixing the name בָּרְכוּ at the top of the display.

LESSON 4 • מַעֲרִיב עֲרָבִים/יוֹצֵר אוֹר

TEXT PAGES 21-25

About the Prayer

There are two blessings which come before the שְׁמַע. In the *morning*, the first of these two blessings is יוֹצֵר אוֹר; in the *evening* the first of these blessings is מַעֲרִיב עֲרָבִים. The יוֹצֵר אוֹר and מַעֲרִיב עֲרָבִים blessings express thanks for the wonders of creation, including light and darkness. The first sentence of יוֹצֵר אוֹר is based on Isaiah 45: 7, "who forms light and creates darkness, who makes peace and creates evil." When composing the prayer, however, the rabbis changed the last word of this biblical verse from "evil," to "all things."

Essential Question

Why be thankful for daytime and for nighttime?

Learning Objectives

Learners will be able to:

- Identify יוֹצֵר אוֹר and מַעֲרִיב עֲרָבִים as the first blessings before the שְׁמַע, in the morning and the evening respectively.
- Recite יוֹצֵר אוֹר and מַעֲרִיב עֲרָבִים.
- Define key words in יוֹצֵר אוֹר and מַעֲרִיב עֲרָבִים.
- Explain that יוֹצֵר אוֹר and מַעֲרִיב עֲרָבִים celebrate the wonder of creation and its renewal each day.
- Recognize that words with the root אוֹר have "light" as part of the word's meaning.
- Locate יוֹצֵר אוֹר in the Shabbat morning service.
- Reflect on why, according to Jewish tradition, we express appreciation for day, night, and the celestial lights.

New Words and Phrases

(H1#6) מַעֲרִיב עֲרָבִים	(H1#10) יוֹצֵר	(H1#14) עֹשֶׂה
(H1#7) חַי	(H1#11) אוֹר	(H1#15) שָׁלוֹם
(H1#8) וְקַיָּם	(H1#12) וּבוֹרֵא	(H1#16) הַכֹּל
(H1#9) יִמְלֹךְ	(H1#13) חֹשֶׁךְ	

Introducing the Lesson

Sit with your class in a circle. Explain that the class will compose a story by going around the circle, each person adding a sentence to the previous person's sentence. The story will be about a day of twenty-four hours of light in which the sun never sets or a day of twenty-four hours of darkness in which the sun never rises.

Get your class started with an opening sentence. Begin by saying, for example: It was about 9 p.m. on a hot day in July, and the sun was still shining brightly overhead. The learner next to you should add the next sentence. Continue until all learners have contributed to the story or you feel the story has reached an interesting point.

Ask: Based on our story, what are some reasons we should appreciate both daylight and nighttime?

Reading Fluency

Ask your education director which lines of מַעֲרִיב עֲרָבִים learners should learn to read fluently. Depending on your school's expectations, you may need to devote time for learners to learn to read all ten lines fluently, or you may have learners learn to read selections from the blessing.

Lines 4–9 contain many unfamiliar words that may be challenging to decode. To make the reading more accessible, ask learners to identify familiar words and/or words that are easy for them to decode. Then, read each line aloud. Have learners read each line after you, before you read the next.

Focus learners on the word בְּחָכְמָה, found on page 21, line 4. Read the word aloud. Ask learners to describe the difference between the pronunciation of the vowel under the ח and the vowel under the מ. (*The first vowel is pronounced "oh"; the second is pronounced "ah."*) Refer learners back to the קִדּוּשׁ in which the ָ is pronounced "oh" at the beginning of both קָדְשׁוֹ and קָדְשְׁךָ.

Collaborative learning can help your learners gain reading fluency. Refer to page 11 for ideas on structuring your lesson so that learners are working together in groups and helping one another become more fluent in reciting יוֹצֵר אוֹר and מַעֲרִיב עֲרָבִים.

Bringing the Prayer to Life

As your learners gain fluency in reciting יוֹצֵר אוֹר and מַעֲרִיב עֲרָבִים, integrate these blessings into your daily, or weekly, classroom service. You may want to alternate the blessings.

Once learners become more fluent in reciting these blessings, have volunteers take turns leading them in your classroom service.

Artistic Expression: Understanding יוֹצֵר אוֹר

Give each learner a sheet of light-colored 9" × 12" construction paper. Have learners fold the paper to form four 4½" × 6" rectangles, and label each rectangle with one of the phrases from this blessing: יוֹצֵר אוֹר; וּבוֹרֵא חֹשֶׁךְ; עֹשֶׂה שָׁלוֹם; וּבוֹרֵא אֶת-הַכֹּל. Provide markers or crayons. Direct learners to illustrate each of these blessing phrases. Invite volunteers to describe their illustrations. Display the illustrations on the bulletin board.

Where We Are

If you have a list displayed of the Shabbat blessings (see page 7), place a marker next to the name יוֹצֵר אוֹר, or write יוֹצֵר אוֹר below בָּרְכוּ.

LESSON 5 • שְׁמַע/וְאָהַבְתָּ
TEXT PAGES 26-32

About the Prayer

The שְׁמַע, which comes from Deuteronomy 6: 4, declares our faith in one unique God. This pledge of our allegiance to God is recited daily in the morning and evening prayers, at bedtime, and as a source of strength in times of sorrow.

The second sentence of the שְׁמַע was first said in the ancient Temple in Jerusalem; it was the response given by the people after hearing the Divine Name pronounced by the High Priests. Later it became the response to the first line of the שְׁמַע. In some congregations, this line is usually recited silently or in a soft voice.

The וְאָהַבְתָּ, taken from Deuteronomy 6: 5-9, reminds us to show love for God by following God's commandments. The וְאָהַבְתָּ tells us to teach Torah to our children, and to affix a mezuzah to our doorpost as a reminder of our respect for God's commandments.

Essential Question

How do we show our love for God and respect for Jewish tradition?

Learning Objectives

Learners will be able to:

- Explain that the שְׁמַע is our pledge of allegiance to God and that the וְאָהַבְתָּ describes ways to show love for God.
- Recite the שְׁמַע, בָּרוּךְ שֵׁם, and the וְאָהַבְתָּ.
- Define key words found in the שְׁמַע, בָּרוּךְ שֵׁם, and the וְאָהַבְתָּ.
- Identify and say the meaning of the root letters מלכ and אהב.
- Recognize that words with the root מלכ have "king" or "ruler" as part of their meaning, and that that words built on the root אהב have "love" as part of their meaning.
- Explain their personal understanding of what it means to "love God."
- Describe traditions associated with reciting the שְׁמַע: covering our eyes, whispering בָּרוּךְ שֵׁם.
- Locate the שְׁמַע and the וְאָהַבְתָּ in the Shabbat morning service.

New Words and Phrases

שְׁמַע (H1#17)
יִשְׂרָאֵל (H1#18)
יְיָ (H1#2)
אֱלֹהֵינוּ (H1#19)
אֶחָד (H1#20)
בָּרוּךְ (H1#4)

שֵׁם (H1#21)
כְּבוֹד (H1#22)
מַלְכוּתוֹ (H1#23)
לְעוֹלָם וָעֶד (H1#5)
וְאָהַבְתָּ (H1#24)
לְבָבְךָ (H1#25)

הַדְּבָרִים (H1#26)
לְאוֹת (H1#27)
מְזֻזוֹת (H1#28)
בֵּיתֶךָ (H1#29)

Introducing the Lesson

INTRODUCING THE שְׁמַע

Ask: If you say to a friend, "Listen to me," what do you want your friend to do? (*hear your words, understand what you are saying, follow your directions*) If you say to a friend, "Do you hear what I'm saying?" What do you want to know? (*if your friend is listening to you; if your friend understands*) Ask your learners When they might say, "I hear you."

Explain that the prayer they are about to study, the שְׁמַע, begins with a word meaning "hear" or "listen." Our tradition teaches that in this prayer we are being commanded to listen to and understand the words of the prayer, not simply to hear the words.

INTRODUCING THE וְאָהַבְתָּ

Direct learners to work in pairs or small groups and to write short responses to these two questions: How do your parents show love for you? (*give us food, arrange for fun experiences*) How do you show love for your parents? (*help with chores, give hugs*)

Introduce and discuss the term "reciprocal love." (*mutual, giving and getting at the same time*) Invite learners to share their responses to the two questions above and to describe how their answers are describing "reciprocal love." (*concern for each other, respect each other*)

Explain that, according to tradition, there is reciprocal love between God and the Jewish people. There are blessings before the שְׁמַע that tell of God's love of us (אַהֲבַת עוֹלָם and אַהֲבָה רַבָּה) and the וְאָהַבְתָּ tells how we can show our love of God.

Roots

To reinforce the concept of Hebrew roots:

- Prepare two trees with roots as described on page 21: One tree for the root מלכ and one for the root אהב.
- Write the English meaning–"ruler, king"–on the trunk of the מ ל כ tree and the English meaning–"love"–on the trunk of the א ה ב tree.
- Write or affix the word מַלְכוּתוֹ on the leafy top of the מ ל כ tree. Add, or invite learners to add, other words with this same root: מֶלֶךְ-מַלְכֵּנוּ-מַלְכָּה-יִמְלֹךְ-מַלְכוּת
- Write or affix the word וְאָהַבְתָּ on the leafy top of the א ה ב tree. Add the names of the two prayers which include the same root letters: אַהֲבַת עוֹלָם-אַהֲבָה רַבָּה

Bringing the Prayer to Life

As your learners gain fluency in reciting the שְׁמַע and the וְאָהַבְתָּ, integrate these prayers into your classroom service and have volunteers take turns leading these prayers. Model covering your eyes as you recite the שְׁמַע. Follow your congregation's tradition of either standing or sitting during the recitation, and of saying the response (בָּרוּךְ שֵׁם) aloud or in a whisper.

Where We Are

If you have a list displayed of the Shabbat blessings (see page 7), place a marker next to the שְׁמַע and the וְאָהַבְתָּ or write שְׁמַע and then וְאָהַבְתָּ below יוֹצֵר אוֹר.

LESSON 6 • מִי כָמֹכָה
TEXT PAGES 33-38

About the Prayer

The מִי כָמֹכָה recalls the biblical account of the Israelites singing a song of praise to God after God brought them out of Egypt, parted the waters of the Sea of Reeds, and made them a free people. Two of the verses in the מִי כָמֹכָה are quotes from this song of praise, the Song of the Sea. (Exodus 15) The מִי כָמֹכָה praises God for the miracle of freeing our ancestors from Egypt and for the gift of freedom.

The מִי כָמֹכָה that includes these ancient verses from the Song of the Sea has become part of our daily morning and evening prayer services. It continues to remind us of our obligation to fulfill the mitzvah of פִּדְיוֹן שְׁבוּיִים – redeeming captives. The blessing concludes by praising God for redeeming Israel.

Essential Questions

Why is it our responsibility to help others to live in freedom?

What is a miracle?

Learning Objectives

Learners will be able to:

- Articulate how the מִי כָמֹכָה is a retelling of the Israelites' celebration of crossing the Sea of Reeds.
- Recite the מִי כָמֹכָה.
- Define key words found in the מִי כָמֹכָה.
- Connect the name מַכַּבִּי to the מִי כָמֹכָה.
- Describe the written format of the Song of the Sea as it appears in a Torah scroll and offer opinions about why it is written in that form.
- Categorize the מִי כָמֹכָה as a prayer of praise, request or thanks.
- Identify the root letters קדשׁ and recognize that words with this root קדשׁ have "holy" or "set apart" as part of their meaning.
- Discuss their personal understanding of awesome events and miracles.
- Locate the מִי כָמֹכָה in the Shabbat morning service.

New Words and Phrases

מִי (H1#30) | יְיָ (H1#2) | בַּקֹּדֶשׁ (H1#34)

כָמֹכָה, כָּמֹכָה (H1#31) | נֶאְדָּר (H1#33)

Introducing the Lesson

Ask: How do you react when something amazing and unexpected happens to you? (*tell friends and family about it; jump up and down; shout*) Explain that, according to tradition, when the Israelites left Egypt and miraculously crossed the Sea of Reeds they sang and danced in joy and thanks. Tell learners that the prayer they are about to study, the מִי כָמֹכָה, expresses gratitude for these miraculous events.

Exploring the Prayer

Ask text-based questions. Questions might include: Which words tell us that the Israelites believe there is no one like Adonai? (*Who is like You–מִי כָמֹכָה*) In lines 2-3, how do the Israelites describe God? (*majestic in holiness–נֶאְדָּר בַּקֹּדֶשׁ; awesome in splendor–נוֹרָא תְהִלֹּת; doing wonders–עֹשֵׂה פֶלֶא*) What did the Israelites say at the shore of the sea? (*Adonai will rule forever–יְיָ יִמְלֹךְ לְעוֹלָם וָעֶד*) In lines 9–14, what terms are used to describe God? (*Rock of Israel–צוּר יִשְׂרָאֵל; our Redeemer–גֹּאֲלֵינוּ; Holy One of Israel–קְדוֹשׁ יִשְׂרָאֵל*)

Challenge learners to find each appearance of יִשְׂרָאֵל in lines 9-14. (*5 times*) Ask: Why do you think יִשְׂרָאֵל appears so many times?

Roots

To reinforce the concept of Hebrew roots:

- Challenge learners to find two words in the מִי כָמֹכָה with the root קדשׁ (בַּקֹּדֶשׁ, קְדוֹשׁ).
- If you have a קדשׁ root tree displayed, add these two words to the tree.

An Ethical Echo

This exercise can serve as a door to Project Based Learning in your classroom. Assist your learners in finding out about Jewish organizations that are working to free people from slavery or other dangerous conditions. You may also want to have your class research and discuss how the Israeli government upholds the mitzvah of פִּדְיוֹן שְׁבוּיִים. The guidelines of the Israel Ministry of Foreign Affairs state that "The Government will do everything in its power to bring about the release of Israeli prisoners of war and missing soldiers, and to bring them back to Israel."

Your learners may be motivated to work as a class in the fight against slavery and dangerous living or working conditions. You can learn more about implementing Project Based Learning in the Supplementary School at www.behrmanhouse.com/project-based-learning.

Bringing the Prayer to Life

Teach learners to chant the מִי כָמֹכָה. Many congregations rise at the beginning of צוּר יִשְׂרָאֵל and remain standing through the recitation of the next prayer, the עֲמִידָה. If your learners know the command, לָקוּם–rise–have them identify the word in line 7 that means "rise." (קוּמָה)

Once learners become more fluent in reciting the מִי כָמֹכָה, have volunteers take turns leading this prayer in your classroom service.

Where We Are

If you have a list displayed of the Shabbat blessings (see page 7), place a marker next to the מִי כָמֹכָה or write מִי כָמֹכָה below וְאָהַבְתָּ.

LESSON 7 • אָבוֹת/אָבוֹת וְאִמָּהוֹת

TEXT PAGES 39-45

About the Prayer

The אָבוֹת וְאִמָּהוֹת, the first blessing of the עֲמִידָה, describes the Jewish people's connection with God in the past, present, and future. This first blessing refers to our patriarchs and matriarchs, reminding us that they believed in God thousands of years ago. Each of our patriarchs and matriarchs had a unique relationship with God. We therefore distinguish each relationship with God by reciting the phrases "God of Abraham, God of Isaac, and God of Jacob, God of Sarah, God of Rebecca, God of Rachel, and God of Leah." The blessing also states that God continues to perform acts of loving-kindness and that God will bring a redeemer or redemption to the Jewish people.

The אָבוֹת וְאִמָּהוֹת includes the concepts and language of Deuteronomy 10: 15–18. These verses from Torah recount how God chose the Jewish people because of the merits of our ancestors, tell of God's loving-kindness, and refer to God as הָאֵל הַגָּדוֹל הַגִּבֹּר וְהַנּוֹרָא. In some congregations, this blessing mentions only the אָבוֹת and not the אִמָּהוֹת.

The Amidah is central to every prayer service. It is recited daily, morning, afternoon, and night. Conservative and Orthodox congregations recite an additional Amidah, called the *Musaf* Amidah, on Shabbat and festival mornings.

Essential Question

What does God's relationship with our patriarchs and matriarchs have to do with us today?

Learning Objectives

Learners will be able to:

- Articulate how the אָבוֹת וְאִמָּהוֹת reflects our relationship to God in the past, present, and future.
- Recite the אָבוֹת וְאִמָּהוֹת, according to the traditions of their own synagogue.
- Define key words found in אָבוֹת וְאִמָּהוֹת.
- Explain the meaning of חֲסָדִים טוֹבִים and give examples of how we can enact this Jewish value.
- Describe when, according to tradition, we bow while reciting the אָבוֹת וְאִמָּהוֹת.
- Locate the אָבוֹת וְאִמָּהוֹת in the Shabbat morning service.

New Words and Phrases

(H2#1) אָבוֹת
(H2#2) אֲבוֹתֵינוּ
(H2#3) אֱלֹהֵי
(H2#4) אַבְרָהָם
(H2#5) יִצְחָק
(H2#6) יַעֲקֹב
(H2#7) אִמָּהוֹת
(H2#8) אִמּוֹתֵינוּ
(H2#9) שָׂרָה
(H2#10) רִבְקָה
(H2#11) לֵאָה
(H2#12) רָחֵל
(H2#13) הַגָּדוֹל
(H2#14) הַגִּבּוֹר
(H2#15) וְהַנּוֹרָא
(H2#16) עֶלְיוֹן
(H2#17) חֲסָדִים טוֹבִים
(H2#18) מֶלֶךְ
(H2#19) עוֹזֵר
(H2#20) וּמוֹשִׁיעַ
(H2#21) וּמָגֵן

Introducing the Lesson

Open the discussion by saying that there are some people, places, or things that are so familiar and/or important that we don't need to use the full name or explain what we mean. For example, when someone in the United States says "the President," everyone knows who that is. Invite learners to provide similar examples of saying "the" plus a noun in place of a full name. (*Suggestions might include: the city; the train; the mall*)

Explain that in this lesson learners will learn the first blessing of a prayer that is so important that one of the prayer's names is simply הַתְּפִלָּה: "the" prayer.

Prayer Variations

Have learners identify which variation of the אָבוֹת or the אָבוֹת וְאִמָּהוֹת is recited in your congregation. Direct learners to circle the phrases or words, such as וּפֹקֵד on page 41 that your congregation includes.

Acts of Loving-Kindness

Have learners locate the phrase חֲסָדִים טוֹבִים on page 39 (*line 6*) or 40 (*line 8*). Explain that חֲסָדִים טוֹבִים are acts of kindness and that we can do an act of kindness for someone rich or poor. Ask: According to the Torah, what are some חֲסָדִים טוֹבִים God has done for the Jewish people? (*Suggestions might include: taken us out of Egypt; given us manna in the desert; given us great leaders like Moses*) What are some חֲסָדִים טוֹבִים we can do for others? (*visit and/or send cards to the sick; invite a new classmate to your home*)

Have your learners look ahead to page 79. Explain that the teaching on this page is sung as part of the Shabbat service in many congregations. Call on a volunteer to read the teaching–"The world rests on three things: on Torah, on worship of God, and on acts of loving-kindness." Ask: Why do you think the rabbis taught that one of the three things the world rests on is loving-kindness? (*to remind us that we all need to help each other; to emphasize that to have a good world we must do acts of loving-kindness; to teach us that helping others is one of the most important things we can do*)

Bringing the Prayer to Life

Once learners become more fluent reciting the אָבוֹת or the אָבוֹת וְאִמָּהוֹת, have volunteers take turns leading this prayer in your classroom service. Have them practice the variation that is recited in your congregation.

Review **Prayer in Motion** on page 45. Encourage learners to practice the choreography of taking steps backward and then forward, and bowing on the words בָּרוּךְ אַתָּה יְיָ at the beginning and end of this blessing. Model how we bend our knees on the word בָּרוּךְ, bow from the waist on the word אַתָּה, and stand up straight when we say God's name, Adonai.

Where We Are

If you have a list displayed of the Shabbat blessings (see page 7), place a marker next to the אָבוֹת or the אָבוֹת וְאִמָּהוֹת or write אָבוֹת or אָבוֹת וְאִמָּהוֹת below מִי כָמֹכָה.

LESSON 8 • גְּבוּרוֹת/קְדוּשָּׁה
TEXT PAGES 46-53

About the Prayer

The גְּבוּרוֹת, the second blessing of the עֲמִידָה, praises God's miraculous powers and expresses the belief that God performs miracles in nature. Declarations of God's power to give life frame the גְּבוּרוֹת. While this is traditionally understood to mean that God gives life to the dead, many Reform and Reconstructionist Jews interpret it to mean that God gives life to everything. The גְּבוּרוֹת details God's marvels as it enumerates the acts of loving-kindness God does for us.

The קְדוּשָּׁה, the third blessing of the עֲמִידָה, declares God's holiness. While there are several versions of the קְדוּשָּׁה, such as the weekday קְדוּשָּׁה and the festival קְדוּשָּׁה, all versions include the same three biblical quotes taken from

Isaiah 6: 3 (קָדוֹשׁ, קָדוֹשׁ, קָדוֹשׁ יְיָ צְבָאוֹת, מְלֹא כָל הָאָרֶץ כְּבוֹדוֹ)

Ezekiel 3: 12 (בָּרוּךְ כְּבוֹד יְיָ מִמְּקוֹמוֹ)

and Psalms 146: 10 (יִמְלֹךְ יְיָ לְעוֹלָם, אֱלֹהַיִךְ צִיּוֹן, לְדֹר וָדֹר, הַלְלוּיָהּ)

The קְדוּשָּׁה, like other prayers that sanctify God, is recited only in the presence of a minyan.

Essential Questions

Why does Jewish tradition teach us that we must be kind and compassionate?

How do we add holiness to our lives? What makes something holy?

Learning Objectives

Learners will be able to:

- Articulate how the גְּבוּרוֹת speaks of God's power to give life, to heal, and to free captives.
- Explain that we declare God's holiness and praise God's glory and greatness when we recite the קְדוּשָּׁה.
- Define key words found in the גְּבוּרוֹת and in the קְדוּשָּׁה.
- Identify and say the meaning of the root letters רחמ, חיה and קדש.
- Recite the גְּבוּרוֹת and the קְדוּשָּׁה as they perform the accompanying movements, according to the traditions of their own synagogue.
- Describe when, according to tradition, we rise on our toes when reciting the קְדוּשָּׁה.
- Locate the גְּבוּרוֹת and the קְדוּשָּׁה in the Shabbat morning service.

New Words and Phrases

אַתָּה (H2#22)
גִּבּוֹר (H2#23)
לְעוֹלָם (H2#24)
מְחַיֵּה (H2#25)
לְהוֹשִׁיעַ (H2#26)
חַיִּים (H2#27)
בְּרַחֲמִים (H2#28)
מִי כָמוֹךָ (H2#29)
נְקַדֵּשׁ (H2#30)
שִׁמְךָ (H2#31)
כְּבוֹדוֹ (H2#32)
יִמְלֹךְ (H2#33)
לְדוֹר וָדוֹר (H2#34)
נַגִּיד (H2#35)
גָּדְלֶךָ (H2#36)

Introducing the Lesson

INTRODUCING THE גְּבוּרוֹת

Ask: Is there someone that you admire that inspires you to do good things? Invite learners to tell about someone who has inspired them to do good things or act in a kinder way. For example, a learner might be motivated to welcome a new classmate because someone welcomed her to a new school. Inform the class that in the גְּבוּרוֹת we find a description of God's powers, such as healing the sick or freeing the captive. As we study the גְּבוּרוֹת, we will look at these powers of God to see how they might inspire us to do good things and act with kindness.

INTRODUCING THE קְדוּשָׁה

When we studied the גְּבוּרוֹת, we spoke about how we can be inspired by the qualities of God as passed down through our tradition. The קְדוּשָׁה tells of God's holiness. In the Torah we are told to be a holy people ("You shall be holy, for I, Adonai, your God, am holy." [Leviticus 19: 2]) What do you think it means to be a holy people? What are some things you might do that reflect that we are a holy people? (*be kind to others, take care of the environment, respect elders*)

Prayer Variations

Have learners identify which variation of the גְּבוּרוֹת and the קְדוּשָׁה is recited in your congregation. Direct learners to circle the phrases or w ords that your congregation includes.

Roots

To reinforce the concept of Hebrew roots:

- Prepare a tree with roots as described on page 21 for the root חיה.
- Write the English meaning–"life"–on the trunk.
- Write or affix the words שֶׁהֶחֱיָנוּ-חַי-מְחַיֵּה-חַיִּים-וּמְחַיֶּה-לְהַחֲיוֹת to the leafy top of the tree.
- If you have a קדשׁ root tree displayed, add these words and the word קְדוּשָׁה.

Bringing the Prayer to Life

Once learners become more fluent reciting the גְּבוּרוֹת and the קְדוּשָׁה, have volunteers take turns leading these prayers in your classroom service. Have them practice the variation that is recited in your congregation. Model how we lift our heels as we say קָדוֹשׁ, קָדוֹשׁ, קָדוֹשׁ. If your congregation bows at the words וְקָרָא זֶה אֶל זֶה, demonstrate the motions by bowing to the left at the words וְקָרָא זֶה and bowing right when saying אֶל זֶה. Encourage learners to practice this choreography.

Where We Are

If you have a list displayed of the Shabbat blessings (see page 7), place a marker next to the גְּבוּרוֹת and the קְדוּשָׁה or write גְּבוּרוֹת and then קְדוּשָׁה below אָבוֹת וְאִמָּהוֹת.

LESSON 9 • בִּרְכַּת שָׁלוֹם: שָׁלוֹם רָב/שִׂים שָׁלוֹם/עֹשֶׂה שָׁלוֹם

TEXT PAGES 54-59

About the Prayer

The final blessing of the עֲמִידָה, בִּרְכַּת שָׁלוֹם, has two versions: שִׂים שָׁלוֹם, recited in the morning, and שָׁלוֹם רָב, recited in the evening. Both versions of בִּרְכַּת שָׁלוֹם are based on the priestly blessing (Numbers 6: 24–26). In both the evening and the morning we close the עֲמִידָה with an additional prayer for peace, עֹשֶׂה שָׁלוֹם. According to the ancient rabbis, because of the supreme value of peace, all prayers should conclude with a prayer for peace. שָׁלוֹם רָב, שִׂים שָׁלוֹם, and עֹשֶׂה שָׁלוֹם all express our yearning for peace for Israel and for the entire world.

שָׁלוֹם is translated as "peace" but it means much more than that. שָׁלוֹם comes from the Hebrew word *shaleim* which means "complete" or "perfect." When we create peace, we are complete and are helping to create a perfect world.

Essential Question

Why, according to Jewish tradition, is peace, shalom, so important?

Learning Objectives

Learners will be able to:

- Explain how בִּרְכַּת שָׁלוֹם expresses our hopes for peace for Israel and all the world.
- Recite שָׁלוֹם רָב, שִׂים שָׁלוֹם, and עֹשֶׂה שָׁלוֹם, as they perform the accompanying physical actions, according to the traditions of their own congregation.
- Define key words and roots found in שָׁלוֹם רָב, שִׂים שָׁלוֹם, and עֹשֶׂה שָׁלוֹם.
- Locate שָׁלוֹם רָב, שִׂים שָׁלוֹם, and עֹשֶׂה שָׁלוֹם in the Shabbat morning service.

New Words and Phrases

(H2#44) שָׁלוֹם
(H2#45) רָב
(H2#46) יִשְׂרָאֵל
(H2#47) עַמְּךָ
(H2#48) וְטוֹב
(H2#49) בְּעֵינֶיךָ
(H2#50) לְבָרֵךְ
(H2#51) בִּשְׁלוֹמֶךָ

(H2#52) שִׂים
(H2#53) טוֹבָה
(H2#54) חֵן
(H2#55) אָבִינוּ
(H2#56) כֻּלָּנוּ כְּאֶחָד
(H2#57) נָתַתָּ
(H2#58) תּוֹרַת חַיִּים
(H2#59) וְאַהֲבַת חֶסֶד

(H2#60) עֹשֶׂה
(H2#61) יַעֲשֶׂה
(H2#62) עָלֵינוּ
(H2#63) וְעַל
(H2#64) כָּל
(H2#65) וְאִמְרוּ
(H2#66) אָמֵן

Introducing the Lesson

Invite learners to describe times when they have saved the best or most important item for last. (*Responses may include: saving their favorite food for last when eating; saving their favorite song for last when listening to music*) When there is a contest, who is generally announced last–the first, second, or third place winner? (*first place*) Discuss how there are many examples of the most important or influential item coming last. Inform learners that the ancient rabbis taught that the greatest Jewish value is peace and that all our prayers should conclude with a prayer for peace. In this lesson, they will study three blessings for peace which are recited at the end of the עֲמִידָה.

Prayer Variations

Have learners identify which variation of שָׁלוֹם רָב, שִׂים שָׁלוֹם, and עֹשֶׂה שָׁלוֹם is recited in your congregation. Direct learners to circle the phrases or words that your congregation includes.

Roots

To reinforce the concept of Hebrew roots:

- Prepare a tree with roots as described on page 21 for the root עשה.
- Write the English meaning–"make"–on the trunk.
- Have learners find the two words in עֹשֶׂה שָׁלוֹם that have this root. (עֹשֶׂה-יַעֲשֶׂה) Direct learners to turn back in their text to page 10 and find another word with this root. (שֶׁעָשָׂה in the Hanukkah blessing, student text page 12) and to look at the Kiddush on page 12 to find one more (לְמַעֲשֵׂה).
- Write or affix the words יַעֲשֶׂה-שֶׁעָשָׂה-עֹשֶׂה-לְמַעֲשֵׂה to the leafy top of the tree.
- Have learners complete the root עשה activity on page 59 with a partner.

Bringing the Prayer to Life

Once learners become more fluent reciting שָׁלוֹם רָב, שִׂים שָׁלוֹם, and עֹשֶׂה שָׁלוֹם, have volunteers take turns leading these prayers in your classroom service. Have them practice the variation that is recited in your congregation. Consider alternating between שִׂים שָׁלוֹם and שָׁלוֹם רָב.

Explain that when we recite עֹשֶׂה שָׁלוֹם it is as if we are symbolically leaving the presence of God at the end of the עֲמִידָה, the way a person would take leave of a king or queen. Demonstrate the choreography for this prayer: take three steps back and then bow to the left as you say עֹשֶׂה, bow to the right as you as הוּא, and bow center front on the word עָלֵינוּ. Have learners practice stepping back and then bowing as they recite this line.

Where We Are

If you have a list displayed of the Shabbat morning blessings (see page 7), place a marker next to שִׂים שָׁלוֹם and עֹשֶׂה שָׁלוֹם or add שִׂים שָׁלוֹם and then עֹשֶׂה שָׁלוֹם below the קְדוּשָּׁה.

LESSON 10 • אֵין כָּמוֹךָ/אַב הָרַחֲמִים/כִּי מִצִּיּוֹן/לְךָ יְיָ

TEXT PAGES 60–66

About the Prayer

אֵין כָּמוֹךָ and אַב הָרַחֲמִים open the Torah service and help prepare us to receive the words of Torah. אֵין כָּמוֹךָ declares that there is none like our God and that God is the eternal Ruler of the Jews. As we recite אַב הָרַחֲמִים, we describe God as a merciful parent and trustworthy ruler. As we prepare to hear the words of the Torah, it is God, not the Torah, which we praise.

Several prayers, כִּי מִצִּיּוֹן, בָּרוּךְ שֶׁנָּתַן, שְׁמַע, גַּדְּלוּ לַייָ and לְךָ יְיָ, are recited as we open the Ark and remove the Torah from the Ark. The words of these prayers link our past to our present and future, honor the Land of Israel and the Torah, and praise God for giving us the Torah.

Essential Questions

How and why do we prepare ourselves to receive the words of Torah?

How are the Land of Israel and the Torah continuing sources of strength to the Jewish people?

Learning Objectives

Learners will be able to:

- Recite אֵין כָּמוֹךָ, אַב הָרַחֲמִים, כִּי מִצִּיּוֹן, בָּרוּךְ שֶׁנָּתַן, שְׁמַע, גַּדְּלוּ לַייָ and לְךָ יְיָ.
- Explain that these prayers affirm our loyalty to God and praise God's greatness.
- Identify אֵין כָּמוֹךָ and אַב הָרַחֲמִים as the opening prayers of the Torah service.
- Describe the choreography associated with removing the Torah from the Ark, according to the customs of their own congregation.
- Define key words from these prayers.
- Identify the root letters מלכ, and רחמ and recognize the meaning of words with these roots.
- Locate כִּי מִצִּיּוֹן, בָּרוּךְ שֶׁנָּתַן, שְׁמַע, גַּדְּלוּ לַייָ and לְךָ יְיָ in the Shabbat morning service.

New Words and Phrases

(H3#1) אֵין	(H3#7) מָלָךְ	(H3#13) תּוֹרָה
(H3#2) כָּמוֹךָ	(H3#8) יִמְלֹךְ	(H3#14) וּדְבַר
(H3#3) (כְּ)מַעֲשֶׂיךָ	(H3#9) הָרַחֲמִים	(H3#15) מִירוּשָׁלָיִם
(H3#4) מַלְכוּתְךָ	(H3#10) יְרוּשָׁלָיִם	(H3#16) שֶׁנָּתַן
(H3#5) וּמֶמְשַׁלְתְּךָ	(H3#11) בָּטָחְנוּ	(H3#17) לְעַמּוֹ
(H3#6) מֶלֶךְ	(H3#12) מִצִּיּוֹן	(H3#18) בִּקְדֻשָּׁתוֹ

Introducing the Lesson

Visit your congregation's sanctuary with your class. Have learners gather around the Ark. Talk about its design and any English or Hebrew wording that appears on or above the Ark. Open the Ark and invite your learners to describe and ask questions about the Torah, its garments, and ornaments. Ask: Why do you think there is a set place to keep a Torah? Why do you think we put a beautiful cover and ornaments on a Torah?

Before you head back to class, tell learners that they are about to learn several short prayers that are part of the ceremony of taking the Torah out of the Ark before we read from the Torah. Back in the classroom, explain that you want everyone to think about what they just saw and about the ideas and words in prayers they have already studied. If you have root trees on display, suggest that learners look at the roots that appear in many of our prayers. Have learners work with a partner or in a small group. Give each pair or group a sheet of paper to write their answer to the following: If you were to write a prayer to recite as we take the Torah out of the Ark, what are some ideas, words or roots you would include in the prayer?

Have learners share their answers with the class. Display the answers. As your class studies this lesson, look for and put a check next to any ideas, words, or roots listed by learners that appear in these prayers. For example, if any learners included "use the root letters קדשׁ," put a check next to that listing.

Prayer Variations

Some congregations add either the verse beginning with וַיְהִי בִּנְסֹעַ הָאָרֹן or with הָבוּ גֹדֶל. Have learners identify which variation is recited in your congregation. Direct learners to circle the verse that your congregation includes.

Roots

To reinforce the concept of Hebrew roots:

- If you have root trees on display, challenge learners to look for new words with the roots on display. Add the following: ברכ: יְבָרֵךְ; מלכ: מַלְכוּתְךָ-מָלָךְ-הַמַּמְלָכָה; קדשׁ: בִּקְדֻשָּׁתוֹ; עשׂה: כְּמַעֲשֶׂיךָ.
- Prepare a tree with roots as described on page 21 for the root רחמ.
- Write the English meaning–"mercy, compassion"–on the trunk.
- Write or affix these words to the leafy top of the tree:
  רַחֲמִים-בְּרַחֲמִים-וְרַחֲמִים-הָרַחֲמִים-הָרַחֲמָן-הַמְרַחֵם רַחֵם-בְּרַחֲמָיו-וְרַחוּם.

Bringing the Prayer to Life

As learners become more fluent reciting each of these new prayers, add the prayer to your classr oom service and have volunteers take turns leading these prayers. Have them practice the variation that is recited in your congregation.

Consider setting up an "Ark" in your classroom that holds a miniature facsimile of a Torah. Model how and when the Torah is taken from the Ark and marched around the congregation. To help learners become comfortable with the choreography of taking the Torah from the Ark, encourage the prayer leader to practice this choreography.

Where We Are

If you have a list displayed of the Shabbat morning blessings (see page 7), place a marker next to אֵין כָּמוֹךָ אַב הָרַחֲמִים, כִּי מִצִּיּוֹן, and לְךָ יְיָ or add these prayers below עֹשֶׂה שָׁלוֹם.

LESSON 11 • בִּרְכוֹת הַתּוֹרָה/בִּרְכוֹת הַהַפְטָרָה
TEXT PAGES 67–74

About the Prayer

We recite blessings both before and after each section of the Torah portion is read. The first blessing opens with the בָּרְכוּ, and then praises God for choosing the Jewish people to receive the gift of the Torah. The second blessing, recited after the Torah reader completes the section, praises God for giving us the Torah of truth and eternal life.

The *Haftarah* reading is a selection taken from the Prophets, the second section of the Bible. The prophets were spokespeople for God. They lived and preached over a period of about 750 years–from the time the people of Israel entered Canaan, around 1250 BCE, until shortly after the Israelites returned from exile in Babylonia. The prophets brought hope to the people in times of despair. When the people strayed from the teachings of the Torah, the prophets chastised them to lead them back to God and *mitzvot*.

We recite one blessing before the *Haftarah* reading, and four blessings after the reading. In these blessings, we praise God for the prophets of truth, the Torah, worship, and Shabbat.

Essential Question

What do we learn about the Torah and *Haftarah* from the blessings, honors, and traditions that accompany their reading?

Learning Objectives

Learners will be able to:

- Recite בִּרְכוֹת הַתּוֹרָה and בִּרְכוֹת הַהַפְטָרָה.
- Define key words and the root נתנ.
- Identify trope marks in a Torah or *Haftarah* passage
- Explain that בִּרְכוֹת הַתּוֹרָה praise God for giving us the Torah and that the *Haftarah* blessings praise God for giving us the prophets, the Torah, worship, and Shabbat.
- Describe the choreography associated with reciting the Torah blessings.
- Use synagogue terms, such as פָּרָשָׁה, עֲלִיָּה, and הַפְטָרָה.
- Locate בִּרְכוֹת הַתּוֹרָה and בִּרְכוֹת הַהַפְטָרָה in the Shabbat morning service.

New Words and Phrases

בָּחַר (H3#19)	נוֹתֵן (H3#26)	הַנֶּאֱמָרִים (H3#33)
בָּנוּ (H3#20)	תּוֹרַת (H3#27)	בֶּאֱמֶת (H3#34)
מִכָּל (H3#21)	אֱמֶת (H3#28)	הַבּוֹחֵר (H3#35)
הָעַמִּים (H3#22)	וְחַיֵּי (H3#29)	עַבְדּוֹ (H3#36)
וְנָתַן (H3#23)	עוֹלָם (H3#30)	עַמּוֹ (H3#37)
לָנוּ (H3#24)	(בִּ)נְבִיאִים (H3#31)	וָצֶדֶק (H3#38)
תּוֹרָתוֹ (H3#25)	טוֹבִים (H3#32)	

Introducing the Lesson

INTRODUCING בִּרְכוֹת הַתּוֹרָה

Ask: What are some ways that you can honor someone or let them know that they deserve something special? (*e.g., praise a person–either in writing or verbally; give someone a gift; have them sit in a special place, a seat of honor*) Explain that, according to Jewish tradition, one of the ways we honor people is by calling them up to recite the Torah blessings. This lesson opens with the blessings that a person being honored recites before and after the Torah reading.

INTRODUCING בִּרְכוֹת הַהַפְטָרָה

Invite learners to tell of a time when they spoke up against others or did something that was not popular because they knew it was the right thing to do. A learner might describe, for example, sticking up for a classmate who was being bullied. Explain that, in biblical times, the prophets instructed our ancestors in the Torah's lessons of right and wrong. We continue to study these lessons of the prophets each week when we read the *Haftarah*. In the second part of this lesson, learners will be introduced to the blessings before and after the *Haftarah* reading.

Prayer Variations

In place of the phrase אֲשֶׁר בָּחַר־בָּנוּ מִכָּל־הָעַמִּים, Reconstructionist prayer books use the phrase אֲשֶׁר קֵרְבָנוּ לַעֲבוֹדָתוֹ "who has drawn us to Your service." If your congregation recites the latter phrase, have learners make a note near line 5 on page 67 to use the phrase on page 68.

Roots

To reinforce the concept of Hebrew roots:

- If you have root trees on display, challenge learners to look for new words with the roots on display. Add the following: מלכ: וּבְמַלְכוּת; קדש: לְקַדְּשָׁה; עשה: וְעֹשֶׂה; חיה: וְחַיֵּי; רחמ: וְרַחֲמָן.
- Prepare a tree with roots as described on page 21 for the root נתנ.
- Write the English meaning–"give"–on the trunk.
- Write or affix the words שֶׁנָּתַתָּ-נָתַתָּ-שֶׁנָּתַן-וְנָתַן-נוֹתֵן-נָתַן-יִתֵּן-וּתְנוּ to the leafy top of the tree. Explain that first letter נ and the last letter נ from the root may drop out of the word (e.g., the third root letter נ has dropped out of the word נָתַתָּ).

Bringing the Prayer to Life

As learners become more fluent reciting בִּרְכוֹת הַתּוֹרָה and בִּרְכוֹת הַהַפְטָרָה, add these blessings to your classroom service, using the variation that is recited in your congregation. You may want to have the class recite these chorally, giving everyone an opportunity to practice.

Consider enacting a Torah service on a regular basis until your learners are comfortable with the motions, such as touching the words of the Torah, which are part of your congregation's custom.

Where We Are

If you have a list displayed of the Shabbat morning blessings (see page 7), place a marker next to בִּרְכוֹת הַתּוֹרָה and בִּרְכוֹת הַהַפְטָרָה or add these blessings below לְךָ יְיָ. Leave a space to insert וְזֹאת הַתּוֹרָה between בִּרְכוֹת הַתּוֹרָה and בִּרְכוֹת הַהַפְטָרָה.

LESSON 12 • וְזֹאת הַתּוֹרָה/עֵץ חַיִּים הִיא/עַל שְׁלֹשָׁה דְבָרִים

TEXT PAGES 75-81

About the Prayer

After we finish reading from the Torah scroll, an honoree raises the Torah so that we can all see its words. As we look at the words of the Torah, we recite וְזֹאת הַתּוֹרָה declaring that the words of Torah which we just read are the same ones that Moses shared with the Israelites thousands of years ago. The words of this declaration are taken from Deuteronomy 4: 44 and Numbers 9: 23.

As we return the Torah to the Ark, we chant the עֵץ חַיִּים and compare the Torah to a tree of life. The source of עֵץ חַיִּים is Proverbs 3: 17-18.

The teaching עַל שְׁלֹשָׁה דְבָרִים appears in Pirkei Avot 1: 2. Attributed to Simon the Righteous, this famous teaching has become a popular song in the Jewish community, and has become part of the service in many congregations.

Essential Question

How do the teachings of the Torah and the rabbis apply to our lives today?

Learning Objectives

Learners will be able to:

- Recite וְזֹאת הַתּוֹרָה, עֵץ חַיִּים, and עַל שְׁלֹשָׁה דְבָרִים.
- Define key words.
- Explain that these prayers affirm our appreciation of the gift of Torah.
- Discuss the analogy of the Torah to a Tree of Life.
- Reflect on the values of Torah, worship, and acts of kindness.
- Describe the choreography associated with lifting the Torah and returning the Torah to the Ark, according to the customs of your own congregation.
- Use synagogue terms, such as הַגְבָּהָה and גְּלִילָה.
- Locate וְזֹאת הַתּוֹרָה, עֵץ חַיִּים, and עַל שְׁלֹשָׁה דְבָרִים in the Shabbat morning service.

New Words and Phrases

(H3#39) וְזֹאת
(H3#40) שָׂם
(H3#41) מֹשֶׁה
(H3#42) לִפְנֵי
(H3#43) בְּנֵי
(H3#44) יִשְׂרָאֵל
(H3#45) עֵץ
(H3#46) חַיִּים
(H3#47) מְאֻשָּׁר
(H3#48) דְּרָכֶיהָ
(H3#49) דַּרְכֵי
(H3#50) נֹעַם
(H3#51) שָׁלוֹם
(H3#52) עַל
(H3#53) שְׁלֹשָׁה
(H3#54) דְּבָרִים
(H3#55) הָעוֹלָם
(H3#56) עוֹמֵד
(H3#57) הַתּוֹרָה
(H3#58) הָעֲבוֹדָה
(H3#59) גְּמִילוּת חֲסָדִים

Introducing the Lesson

INTRODUCING וְזֹאת הַתּוֹרָה

Invite learners to imagine that they are setting up an exhibit in a museum and that their job is to write a description of a Torah that will be on display. Have learners work with a partner or in a small group to complete the description of the Torah that begins with the words: This is the Torah that... Ask learners to share their descriptions. Direct learners to open to page 75 and to read aloud the English translation of וְזֹאת הַתּוֹרָה. Ask: How is this description different or similar to what you wrote? What do you think of this description of the Torah?

INTRODUCING עֵץ חַיִּים הִיא

On the board, write: עֵץ חַיִּים הִיא–Tree of Life. Divide the class into groups of three to four learners. Ask each group to list three to five ways that a tree gives us life. After a few minutes, have groups share their lists. Write their suggestions on the board. Ask: Why do you think the Torah has been compared to a Tree of Life? Direct learners to open to page 77 and read the introduction which gives examples of how the Torah is a Tree of Life.

INTRODUCING על שְׁלֹשָׁה דְבָרִים

Materials needed: Three 6"-8" sticks (or pens or markers) of equal length, a small ball or container lid. Invite four volunteers to come to the front of the room. Give each volunteer one of the four items. Direct the volunteers to hold the sticks up so that the ball or container lid balances on the sticks, similar to a three-legged table. Now invite another volunteer to remove any one of the sticks. Discuss how we need at least three supports for something to remain in balance and standing.

Invite learners to turn to page 79. Ask: According to the rabbis, what are the three things that the world needs to stand on?

Bringing the Prayer to Life

As learners become more fluent reciting וְזֹאת הַתּוֹרָה and עֵץ חַיִּים, add these prayers to your classroom service. Also add עַל שְׁלֹשָׁה דְבָרִים if it is recited in your congregation.

Consider enacting a Torah service. Your class can use a miniature Torah to practice holding the Torah high as they sing וְזֹאת הַתּוֹרָה. Model how the Ark is opened and we stand as we sing עֵץ חַיִּים.

Where We Are

If you have a list displayed of the Shabbat morning blessings (see page 7), place a marker next to וְזֹאת הַתּוֹרָה and עֵץ חַיִּים הִיא, or add וְזֹאת הַתּוֹרָה below בִּרְכוֹת הַתּוֹרָה, and עֵץ חַיִּים הִיא below בִּרְכוֹת הַהַפְטָרָה.

LESSON 13 • עָלֵינוּ
TEXT PAGES 82–85

About the Prayer

The עָלֵינוּ is a pledge of our loyalty to God in which we praise God as the one Creator and Ruler. It was added to the Rosh Hashanah service in the third century CE and about a thousand years later became part of every daily prayer service. The closing words of the עָלֵינוּ are taken from the prophet Zechariah. (14: 9)

Essential Question

How do we demonstrate our loyalty to God and the Jewish community?

Learning Objectives

Learners will be able to:

- Explain that the עָלֵינוּ is a pledge of loyalty to God, the one Creator and Ruler.
- Recite the עָלֵינוּ and demonstrate its traditional choreography.
- Define key words found in the עָלֵינוּ.
- Reflect on the value of praying with a community.
- Identify the version of the עָלֵינוּ recited in their congregation.
- Locate the עָלֵינוּ in the Shabbat morning service.

New Words and Phrases

עָלֵינוּ (H3#60)
לְשַׁבֵּחַ (H3#61)
(לַ)אֲדוֹן (H3#62)
הַכֹּל (H3#63)
וַאֲנַחְנוּ (H3#64)
וּמוֹדִים (H3#65)
מֶלֶךְ מַלְכֵי הַמְּלָכִים (H3#66)
הָאָרֶץ (H3#67)
בַּיּוֹם הַהוּא (H3#68)
יִהְיֶה (H3#69)

Introducing the Lesson

Ask: Think about different people, groups, organizations, or places in your life. Which of these are you loyal to? (*Responses may include: parents, a baseball team, friends.*) Why are you loyal to them? How do you show your loyalty?

Inform learners that the prayer they are about to study, the עָלֵינוּ, declares our loyalty to God.

Direct learners' attention to the two letter ending of עָלֵינוּ. Explain that this ending means "us," or "we," and that many words in the עָלֵינוּ have this suffix. The frequent use of "us" and "we" in the עָלֵינוּ also reminds us of our loyalty to others in our community.

Prayer Variations

Invite learners to read **Prayer Variations** on page 83 in the textbook. Then ask them to read lines 3-7 on page 82 and compare these lines to those found in the Reconstructionist prayer book. Ask: Which version do you prefer? Why? Does our congregation use either of these versions?

If your congregation uses *Mishkan T'filah, identify* the version(s) recited in your congregation. Consider having your learners compare the different versions included in this prayer book.

Roots

To reinforce the concept of Hebrew roots:

If you have root trees on display, challenge learners to look for new words with the roots on display. Add the following: מלכ: מַלְכֵי, הַמְּלָכִים; עשה: עָשָׂנוּ; נתנ: לָתֵת.

Praying Together

Have learners work with a partner to complete the Praying Together activity on page 85. Inform learners that many of our prayers and blessings include words with this same suffix נוּ. Assign each pair a blessing or prayer, and challenge them to find and count the number of words with this suffix. The following blessings and prayers that have words with this suffix can be found in the student text on the pages indicated:

שֶׁהֶחֱיָנוּ (page 5); blessing over Shabbat candles (page 6); קִדּוּשׁ (page 12); קְדוּשָּׁה (page 50); שִׂים שָׁלוֹם (page 56); blessings before (page 67) and after (page 69) the Torah reading, second, third, and fourth blessings after the *Haftarah* reading (page 74).

Invite pairs to share how many words they found with the suffix נוּ. Ask: What do you learn from the fact that there are so many words with the suffix נוּ in our prayers and blessings?

Bringing the Prayer to Life

As learners become more fluent reciting the עָלֵינוּ, add it to your classroom service, using the variation that is recited in your congregation. Model how we bend our knees at the word כּוֹרְעִים, bow slightly as we say וּמִשְׁתַּחֲוִים וּמוֹדִים, and then stand straight at the word לִפְנֵי.

Where We Are

If you have a list displayed of the Shabbat morning blessings (see page 7), place a marker next to the עָלֵינוּ or add this prayer below עֵץ חַיִּים.

LESSON 14 • קַדִּישׁ

TEXT PAGES 86-89

About the Prayer

The קַדִּישׁ praises God and expresses our hope that God's laws will bring peace throughout the world. There are a variety of versions of the קַדִּישׁ recited in each prayer service. The קַדִּישׁ often distinguishes the end of one part of a service from the beginning of the next. One version, the Mourner's קַדִּישׁ, is recited at the end of the service in memory of loved ones who have died. The קַדִּישׁ is written in Aramaic, the language spoken by Jews in the fifth century BCE and for about a thousand years after that. The קַדִּישׁ makes no mention of death.

Essential Question

How might the tradition of reciting the Mourner's קַדִּישׁ strengthen connections among the Jewish community?

Learning Objectives

Learners will be able to:

- Recite the קַדִּישׁ.
- Define key words and the root גדל.
- Match Aramaic words of the קַדִּישׁ to related Hebrew words.
- Explain that the קַדִּישׁ, recited by mourners, praises God and doesn't mention death.
- Demonstrate how we bow when reciting עֹשֶׂה שָׁלוֹם at the end of the קַדִּישׁ.
- Locate the Mourner's קַדִּישׁ in the Shabbat morning service.

New Words and Phrases

קַדִּישׁ (H3#70)
יִתְגַּדַּל (H3#71)
וְיִתְקַדַּשׁ (H3#72)
שְׁמֵהּ (H3#73)
בְּעָלְמָא (H3#74)

וְיַמְלִיךְ (H3#75)
מַלְכוּתֵהּ (H3#76)
וּבְחַיֵּי (H3#77)
לְעָלַם (H3#78)

וְיִשְׁתַּבַּח (H3#79)
בְּרִיךְ (H3#80)
בִּרְכָתָא (H3#81)
שְׁלָמָא (H3#82)

Introducing the Lesson

Invite learners to think about prayers and blessings they have studied. As a class, brainstorm a list of things we might say to praise God. Write learners' suggestions on the board. Inform learners that the prayer they are about to study, which praises God, is the prayer recited in memory of someone who has died. Ask: Are you surprised that the prayer we recite in someone's memory praises God and makes no mention of death? Why or why not?

Roots

To reinforce the concept of Hebrew roots:

If you have root trees on display, challenge learners to look for new words with the roots on display. Add the following to the root trees: קדשׁ: קַדִּישׁ, וְיִתְקַדַּשׁ, דְּקֻדְשָׁא; ברכ: מְבָרַךְ, יִתְבָּרַךְ, בְּרִיךְ, בִּרְכָתָא; מלכ: וְיַמְלִיךְ, מַלְכוּתֵהּ; חיה: בְּחַיֵּיכוֹן, וּבְחַיֵּי, וְחַיִּים.

On page 88 of the text, learners are asked to write the meaning of any three of the roots listed from the קַדִּישׁ. If you have root trees displayed, they will readily find the meanings for ברכ, קדשׁ, and מלכ.

While they have learned words with the roots גדל and שׁלמ, they have not focused on these roots. For the root גדל, you can refer learners to the following words and text pages to help them derive that words with this root have "great" as part of their meaning: הַגָּדוֹל, "the great" (page 39, page 40); גָּדְלֶךָ, "your greatness" (page 50); גֹּדֶל, "greatness" (page 64); גָּדוֹל, "great" (page 66); הַגְּדֻלָּה, "the greatness" (page 66); יִתְגַּדַּל, "be great" (page 86). For the root שׁלמ, refer learners to page 55 which explains that the root שׁלמ tells us that "peace," "harmony," "completedness," or "wholeness" is part of a word's meaning.

Building Fluency

The קַדִּישׁ is packed with many unfamiliar words and learners will need gentle, but directed, guidance in mastering this prayer. Introduce a limited number of new lines at a time. For example, read three to four lines of the קַדִּישׁ, phrase by phrase, then line by line, having learners chorally repeat each phrase, and line. Direct learners to read the Hebrew lines with a partner. Walk around the room listening to learners read.

Take note of the words that are most difficult, such as כִרְעוּתֵה, for learners to decode. Practice these challenging words. Encourage learners to ask for assistance in reading difficult words.

After learners have been introduced to all of the קַדִּישׁ, have them practice reading following the jigsaw approach described on page 12. Note: While groups are practicing, you may choose to work one-on-one with learners who need more attention.

Bringing the Prayer to Life

Given that the קַדִּישׁ is said in memory of a loved one, learners may be more comfortable practicing this prayer for fluency, rather than having it a regular part of their class service. Model, and have learners practice, how we take steps back and then bow as we say עֹשֶׂה שָׁלוֹם. Your learners may be become familiar with the Mourner's קַדִּישׁ when they attend services with the main congregation.

Discuss if it is the custom in your congregation for everyone to stand for the Mourner's קַדִּישׁ or if only the mourners stand.

The reality is that there may be a time when a close relative of one of your learners passes away and the family is sitting shiva. Consider encouraging learners to attend the shiva minyan. While the learners will not count as part of the community, they can experience the power of communal support as the mourners recite the קַדִּישׁ.

Where We Are

If you have a list displayed of the Shabbat morning blessings (see page 7), place a marker next to the Mourner's קַדִּישׁ or add this prayer below the עָלֵינוּ.

LESSON 15 • אֵין כֵּאלֹהֵינוּ
TEXT PAGES 90-93

About the Prayer

אֵין כֵּאלֹהֵינוּ is a hymn that describes God as our Sovereign, our Ruler, and our Savior who is beyond compare. It is written in the form of an acrostic, with the first letters of each verse spelling the word אָמֵן. In אֵין כֵּאלֹהֵינוּ we speak as a community about our God. It is sung with spirit and joy at the conclusion of the Shabbat morning service.

Essential Question

How might joining in joyful songs of prayer impact on our connection to the Jewish community?

Learning Objectives

Learners will be able to:

- Recite אֵין כֵּאלֹהֵינוּ.
- Define key words.
- Demonstrate that the first letters of אֵין כֵּאלֹהֵינוּ spell the word אָמֵן.
- Identify and define the prefixes and suffixes in אֵין כֵּאלֹהֵינוּ.
- Explain that אֵין כֵּאלֹהֵינוּ describes God as our Sovereign, our Ruler, and our Savior who is beyond compare.
- Locate אֵין כֵּאלֹהֵינוּ in the Shabbat morning service.

New Words and Phrases

(H3#83) אֵין כּ	(H3#86) אַתָּה הוּא	(H3#89) מַלְכֵּנוּ
(H3#84) מִי כ	(H3#87) אֱלֹהֵינוּ	(H3#90) מוֹשִׁיעֵנוּ
(H3#85) נוֹדֶה ל	(H3#88) אֲדוֹנֵינוּ	

Introducing the Lesson

Invite learners to describe a situation in which they told someone, more than once and in more than one way, that what they did was great. A learner might, for example, describe telling a teammate who scored the winning point for the team how great that person is, how much the person does for the team, and how amazing the play was. Ask: Why did you praise the person in so many different ways? Wasn't it enough to just say once that what they did was great?

Invite learners to think about all the different prayers and blessings they have learned. Ask: Why do you think that after all the prayers and blessings we have recited in our service, we conclude the service by praising God with another hymn of praise? (*Responses may include: because there are so many things for which we want to praise God; because we want to show our appreciation; because it represents that there is no end to our praise for God.*) Inform learners that they will be studying אֵין כֵּאלֹהֵינוּ, a hymn filled with praises of God.

Roots

To reinforce the concept of Hebrew roots:

Challenge learners to identify words with the root מלכ. If you have created a word tree for the root מלכ (see page 21), add the words כְּמַלְכֵּנוּ, כְמַלְכֵּנוּ, לְמַלְכֵּנוּ, and מַלְכֵּנוּ to the tree.

Word Parts

Have learners silently read אֵין כֵּאלֹהֵינוּ.

Ask: What are the four ways we describe God in אֵין כֵּאלֹהֵינוּ? *אֱלֹהֵינוּ – our God, אֲדוֹנֵינוּ – our Sovereign, מַלְכֵּנוּ – our Ruler, מוֹשִׁיעֵנוּ – our Savior*) What do you notice about the consonants and vowels when a prefix or suffix is added? (*the vowels may change, a final letter may drop out*)

Call on a volunteer to identify and translate the word-prefix combination that repeats in lines 1-4. (אֵין כּ- – *there is none like*) Challenge learners to turn back to page 60 and to identify the two phrases that include this same word-prefix combination. (אֵין כָּמוֹךָ *and* וְאֵין כְּמַעֲשֶׂיךָ)

Ask learners to look at lines 5-6 and to name the word-prefix combination that appears in these lines and to say its meaning? (*מִי כ- – who is like*) Challenge learners to name two other prayers that have phrases that begin with this word-prefix combination. (מִי כָמֹכָה-מִי-כָמֹכָה, מִי כָּמֹכָה; גְּבוּרוֹת-מִי כָמוֹךָ)

Call on a learner to identify and translate the word-prefix combination that repeats in lines 7-10. (נוֹדֶה ל – *we will give thanks to*) Challenge learners to name prayer words that begin with the prefix -ל, meaning "to." (לְעַמּוֹ, לָנוּ, לְכָבוֹד, לְשַׁבֵּחַ, לַאֲדוֹן,)

Bringing the Prayer to Life

As learners become more fluent reciting אֵין כֵּאלֹהֵינוּ, add it to your classroom service.

Where We Are

If you have a list displayed of the Shabbat morning blessings (see page 7), place a marker next to אֵין כֵּאלֹהֵינוּ or add this prayer below the Mourner's קַדִּישׁ.

NOTES